Jewish Contributions to the American Way of Life

Asher B. Etkes
Saul Stadtmauer

Northside Publishing Inc.

AUTHORS' NOTE

All things were considered when planning our salute to American Jews who have contributed to the evolution, prosperity and spirit of our nation's way of life. Who did we select and why?

We have confined our biographical reviews to immigrant and native-born Jewish men and women who lived all or a portion of their lives in America during the 20th Century. For perspective, we have also mentioned Jews of earlier times who played meaningful roles in the past history of our country's society and culture.

The people who appear here are broadly defined as being Jewish or of Jewish origins. In keeping with accepted tradition we have also included converts, as well as persons who have abandoned Judaism for other faiths. We hope you will be inspired and take pride in what they have achieved for themselves and for our nation.

Cover and Book Design by Thomas G. Carren

Library of Congress Catalog Card Number 95-069303
ISBN 0-9644430-1-5

Printed in the United States of America
First Edition

This book is available for special sales promotions, fund raising, bulk purchases or educational uses. For further information, contact:

Northside Publishing Inc.
41-04 35th Avenue
Long Island City, NY 11101

Acknowledgements

Our deep appreciation to the many whose various contributions have helped advance this book, among whom are Charlene Soltz, Reed Margulis, Helen Terzian, Patricia Newmark-Carren, Marilyn Wilson, John and Anita Sniderman, Gail Carotenuto, Ed Pitchon, Helen Papagianis and Colette Inez.

Mark Twain, speaking of the Jews:

If the statistics are right, the Jews constitute but one quarter of one percent of the human race. It suggests a nebulous dim puff of stardust lost in the blaze of the Milky Way. Properly, the Jew ought hardly to be heard of; but he is heard of, has always been heard of. He is as prominent on the planet as any other people, and his importance is extravagantly out of proportion to the smallness of his bulk.

His contributions to the world's list of great names in literature, science, art, music, finance, medicine and abstruse learning are very out of proportion to the weakness of his numbers. He has made a marvelous fight in this world in all ages; and has done it with his hands tied behind him. He could be vain of himself and be excused for it. The Egyptians, the Babylonians and the Persians rose, filled the planet with sound and splendour, then faded to dream-stuff and passed away; the Greeks and the Romans followed and made a vast noise, and they are gone; other peoples have sprung up and held their torch high for a time but it burned out, and they sit in twilight now, or have vanished.

The Jew saw them all, survived them all, and is now what he always was, exhibiting no decadence, no infirmities of age, no weakening of his parts, no slowing of his energies, no dulling of his alert and aggressive mind. All things are mortal but the Jew; all other forces pass, but he remains. What is the secret of his immortality?

Harper's magazine, September 1897

President William Howard Taft, speaking of the Jews:

Jews are unique in that for eighteen hundred years they have had no country...and have, whenever there was any pretense of equality of opportunity for them, forged their way ahead into positions of prominence, influence and power in business, professions, in philosophy, in art, in literature, and in government.

The harshest persecution and injustice merely strengthen the peculiarity of the Jew in the adherence to his ancient customs . . .

Give him the sunlight of freedom and the balmy encouragement of equality of opportunity and he assimilates himself to his environment with all the quickness of perception, all the energy, all the enterprise, all the persistence with which he is so remarkably endowed.

From the East End of New York and through centers of population in that country where Jews are gathered by the million and hundreds of thousands come the youth who soon manifest a spirit of Americanism and get on.

Excerpted from:
The National Geographic Magazine, July 1919

CONTENTS

One
The Path to America

Freedom, opportunity and education suggest why American Jews of the 20th Century have risen to prominence in our nation's many enterprises. Although they are relatively few in number, their achievements are the pride of our country . . . in the arts, sciences, entertainment and education, in social, literary and business life. But the journey was long.

The four-thousand year history of Jewry is a story of dislocation and survival against heavy odds. Repressions and expulsions, inhumanity and indignities from the days of the Diaspora have shaped the character of the Jew, the hapless wanderer.

Self protective and often reclusive, yet energetic and enterprising, Jews without nationhood have lived in fragile dependency on foreign hosts. When admitted by them, it was only as disposable guests. Jews endured under harsh restrictions and practiced the few crafts and trades open to them. They were strangers in strange lands, a people without roots, with few hopes for their children's future.

While scattered to the winds, Jews kept their religious and cultural identity intact over the centuries. Why was this?

In the Beginning

According to biblical lore, Abraham from the land of Ur, a site now in Iraq, entered a covenant with God, pledging faith and obedience. Abraham and his heirs were the Chosen – chosen from among the pagans to serve His world as *examples* in thoughts and deeds of moral and righteous people.

The accord between God and Abraham's kin was not a doctrine of racial privilege or superiority. Nor did it command Jews to recruit converts. It implied a duty, as in an old Jewish prayer, "to perfect the world under the rule of God." By example, and that alone.

After generations of slavery in Egypt, the Exodus brought the ancient Israelites an exhilarating taste of milk and honey after an arid pilgrimage to the Promised Land – their first taste of freedom flowering under the Ten Commandments and Mosaic Law.

With a land of their own, they were free to create a social system following a rational code of ethical conduct. These principles, the laws that governed relationships between man and man and between man and God, were new to the ancient world. The beliefs of Jewish monotheism influenced others, and were later embraced by the founders of Christianity and Islam.

Jesus, the rabbi of the New Testament, transmitted this legacy through his teachings. With the exception of Luke, the authors of the New Testament were all Jewish and spiritually informed by their creed.

The chronicle continues. The once powerful northern kingdom of Israel was defeated by the Assyrians in 722 B.C.E., and its ten tribes were exiled. Cast out from their homeland, the people vanished into the mists of history; their descendants were likely assimilated into more benign and accepting societies.

The southern kingdom of Judah fell to Babylon in 587 B.C.E., The great temple in Jerusalem built by Solomon was burned, and the tribe's leaders were deported. But after a half century, a dedicated few returned to rebuild their hallowed city and its sacred shrine.

Measured against the ages, the Jews' renewed unity was short-lived. For 500 years, the residents of the north and south dwelled under the hostile administrations of the Greeks and Romans. They precariously retained the social order and religious rites of Jewish fellowship.

The storm struck in 70 C.E., a momentous event that lingers in Jewish consciousness to this day: the destruction of the second temple by the despotic Titus, then a Roman general, who dispersed the Israelites.

The Long Exile

Almost all of the world's ethnic Jews lived under the heel of Christian and Muslim rule during the dark centuries of the Middle Ages. While their enclaves in Europe, the Middle East and Asia where isolated by distance, a cohesion in spirit and practice preserved their unity and sense of community. The links that bound them were their holy books – the Torah, the Talmud and also the Prophets.

These writings were an anchor and a beacon – reaffirming the Jews' common origins and rituals, their possession of the blesséd word of God. They had in hand an unquenchable fire whose warmth and light nourished them in exile. While vulnerable and stripped of worldly goods, itinerant Jews found solace in what could not be stolen from them by enemies and tyrants: the wisdom and mysteries of their sacred texts.

To ponder Torah and Talmud – guides to leading an honorable spiritual, social and physical life – is to bring order and purpose out of chaos. Talmud is, in fact, derived from the Hebrew words "to study."

So, above all, the Jew must cherish and absorb knowledge through literacy and learning. A reverence for education emerged from the habit of study and analysis in Talmudic discourse. This eventually became the foundation of the Jews' present day world-view, their self-esteem and endurance.

Learning nurtures the mind, and the intellects of Jews have for millennia been a source of sustenance, a shield against cultural, moral and physical decay. A life of the mind and love of learning also tends towards right thoughts and actions – and in the vigor of Torah and Talmud, towards concerns for social justice, universal peace and harmony among people.

Moments of Glory

Although Jewish achievements are small footnotes on the

pages of European history, a few bright episodes stand out. The Golden Age of Spanish Jewry, from the 10th through 12th Centuries, saw Jews appointed to governmental offices under the benevolent leadership of Islamic Moors. Among notables who rose in prestige and influence were diplomats, philosophers, poets and physicians. A rich religious and cultural life flourished.

The 12th Century philosopher and physician, Maimonides, authored the immortal *Guide to the Perplexed* among writings and teachings whose authority touched the non-Jewish world.

Jewish astronomers, mathematicians and map makers to Prince Henry the Navigator of Portugal helped plot a course for the nation's trade routes and dominance at sea during the 14th Century.

The 17th through 18th Centuries found court Jews appointed to political posts within German dukedoms, and saw Baruch Spinoza scandalize co-religionists in Amsterdam with his unorthodox philosophical speculations.

What power was held by members of European Jewry during later centuries was limited to a few important professions, to medicine and finance – and Jews served solely at the whim of their sovereign employers. At times, the regents of England, Spain and Poland invited them to apply their wits to managing national treasuries and taxation, often after irresponsible spending had pushed governments toward bankruptcy.

Money handling had long been the province of Jews who were alone permitted to charge interest for lending capital. Under church canon law, usury was sinful, forbidden to all but social outcasts.

But through successful fiscal management, some Jews cautiously entered royal courts, frequently as converts, but seldom with respect or honor. Their very success and visibility incited state-agitated hostility and recriminations as their dependence on the Old World began to lessen.

Toward the Golden Land

It was a watershed year for Spanish Jews . . . 1492. An edict to expel the Jews who refused to renounce their faith was enforced during the month Christopher Columbus set sail for the New World. Ironically, five crewmen of Jewish origin served with the expedition; one among them, interpreter Luis de Torres, was the first in the fleet to set foot on American soil. Years before the Puritans arrived, de Torres was also the first white man to permanently settle in the New World.

Jews escaping the Inquisition raging through Spain were hard pressed to find safe haven. Many fled to the Netherlands and from there to the Dutch possession of Brazil. But the settlers were once again uprooted and dispossessed as Portuguese forces invaded and wrested Brazil from Dutch hands.

Of the refugees, twenty-three boarded ship in Recife, Brazil, for New Amsterdam, later renamed New York. They planted their lives in a primeval territory under the Dutch flag. The seed that took root in 1654 grew into a vigorous community of Jewish traders, merchants and journeymen, some of whom had emigrated from Holland. Among them, Asser Levy gained prominence.

The first Jewish landowner in North America, and an idealistic democrat, Levy fought to win citizenship for all minority colonists. He advocated free trade, helped establish the first synagogue on the continent, and, in ecumenical spirit, contributed toward building the town's first Lutheran Church.

During the early years of the 18th Century, both devout and secular Christian leaders in American society began paying homage to the Bible's moral and ethical values as bedrocks for the budding state. Hebrew Bibles and other tracts were published here, and Jewish studies were taught at colleges such as Harvard.

Pre-Revolution leaders later met and even debated whether Hebrew might replace English as the tongue of the land. Benjamin Franklin, Thomas Jefferson and John Adams urged that the image of the children of Israel escaping Egypt should symbolically appear on the official seal of the United States.

Hebrew words remain written into the university emblems of Columbia, Yale and Dartmouth. And inscribed on the Liberty Bell that tolled freedom and autonomy for the country and its people are words from the Hebrew scriptures: "Proclaim liberty throughout the land unto all the inhabitants thereof."

Several years after the 1776 War of Independence was won, the Jewish congregation of Newport, Rhode Island, received a letter from the country's recently elected president, George Washington:

"May the children of the Stock of Abraham who
dwell in this land continue to merit and enjoy
the good will of the other inhabitants, while
everyone shall sit in safety under his own vine
and fig tree, and there shall be none to make
him afraid."

In the poetic idiom of the bible, and in the name of the United States government, Washington embraced the Jews – bestowing words of friendship and solace on patriots and loyal citizens who also courageously served in our military as officers, soldiers and suppliers. And were it not for the financial wizardry of Haym Salomon, who almost single-handedly helped finance the Revolution, the colonists' army might have collapsed.

A Dawning Era

Another impetus toward universal freedom was gathering in Europe – the French Revolution which in 1789 did much to undermine an article of faith: the primacy of noble birth and the divine right of the aristocracy to rule. Common people, and Jews among them, were further released from the shackles of royal dominion by the French tide sweeping across the Continent, proclaiming the rights of man. The governing structure of that world would eventually yield to the rallying cry of Napoleon's forces: *Liberty, Equality, Fraternity.*

In France and its vanquished territories, free public education and civil service were newly instituted. Jews in occupied lands and provinces worked hard to gain the skills that could place them at the epicenter of government service. Numbers of Jews thrived in a dawning climate of social and political stability, while those who were less advantaged turned their eyes westward.

The Ingathering Begins

The trickle of Jewish migrants to our shores, begun in post-Revolution years, flowed more rapidly through the end of the century and into the next. Many newcomers, principally from Germany, were educated professionals, some from affluent families. Among them were bankers, merchants, entrepreneurs, doctors, scientists and political activists who sensed a wellspring of opportunity in the heady atmosphere of our young, vibrant nation.

Ephraim Hart helped organize the New York Board of Stockbrokers in 1792, the forerunner of the New York Stock Exchange.

Ernestine Rose launched a humanistic crusade on behalf of women and children, crying out for social justice and free public schooling. Spurred by her tireless advocacy, the nation eventually enacted the 19th Amendment granting suffrage to women.

Isaac Hays, an eminent physician of his day, founded the American Medical Association in 1847. He is also noted for setting the high standards that guide medical journalism in America today.

Sampson Simson was the driving force behind the ground-breaking for New York's Mount Sinai Hospital in 1853. A pioneer in research and health care delivery, the medical center continues as a model for similar institutions worldwide.

David Lubin, a Polish-born storekeeper, ran the first mail order house in the United States during the 1870s. Almost three decades later, he formed the International Institute for Agriculture. The global cooperative became a model for the League of Nations.

Adolphus Solomons, a social welfare leader and philanthropist, helped Clara Barton form the American Red Cross in 1881, and for twelve years served as the organization's first vice-president.

Adam Gimbel, a peddler from Bavaria, and his

American-born sons, built a national chain of modern department stores. The first opened its doors in Milwaukee in 1887.

Levi Strauss, a late 19th Century clothier and businessman, attached his given name to a legendary line of trousers that became the gold standard for western wear valued throughout today's world.

Emile Berliner invented a practical alternative to Thomas Edison's phonograph in 1887: the Victor Talking Machine which replaced the cylinder with a disk and sired a vast industry. Ten years earlier, his unique microphone-receiver made the Bell telephone a workable reality. And he fathered the idea of royalty rights for performing artists.

The Doors Fling Open

At the turn of the century, the ocean of Jewish newcomers swelled with a tidal wave of Eastern European emigrants. Between 1905 and 1914, three-quarters of a million Russian Jews were among large contingents sailing from Poland and other nations on the Continent.

Many passed under the shadow of the Statue of Liberty in whose portals were engraved some of the most memorable words in the English language – written by the Jewish poet and novelist, Emma Lazarus. "Give me your tired, your poor,/ Your huddled masses yearning to be free . . ."

What did the new Americans bring with them other than sparse belongings? They brought ambition and resourcefulness, a respect for education and the invincible conviction that, given the chance they would prevail and prosper – if not for themselves, for their children.

They came with an ageless purpose etched in their hearts and minds: to aspire to excellence, responsibility and hard work. They came for acceptance in a congenial, safe oasis, for a new beginning, and found both. They came to a hospitable land of high promise to give of themselves, and have since shared their gifts with fellow Americans and citizens of the world.

Why do we limit these pages to the achievements of

8

Jewish-Americans of the 20th Century? Generations of Jewish immigrants had settled here before, and a few had begun making their successful way into American society. But not until after the turn-of-the-century did the positive influence of the Jewish presence become as pointed and lasting.

During the preceding fifty years, resident Jews had established institutions that would eventually help integrate and absorb their brethren – the multitudes arriving in the early 1900s. Americanized Jews had built an educational support system that newcomers would utilize. And as they debarked on our shores, the immigrants were greeted by kinsmen in organizations and societies which found them housing and employment.

The consolidation and learning experience took years, but in time, a large population of native born and motivated young adults were readied – with parental encouragement – for seeking opportunity in their new land. The times were also hospitable. America was swept by a mushrooming industrial revolution, massive urbanization and cultural ferment. People were needed: large cadres of educated professionals in all disciplines.

The late decades of the 19th Century set the stage which Jews of accomplishment later entered in large number, and it is these whom you will meet.

Two
Music

Since ancient times, Jewish culture has been wedded to music and song. Readings of biblical passages and ritual prayer were sung and chanted to one of the oldest forms of musical notation. The rabbi, the cantor and the instrumentalist known as the klezmer were the chief agents of song in Jewish communities.

By the 19th Century, European Jews were escaping the confinement of ghettos as residential barriers against them slowly lifted. Some integrated into a growing middle class – into fertile soil for cultivating composers and performers whose folk music evolved along classical and popular lines. The immortal Felix Mendelssohn was the most famous, joined by Johann Strauss, Jacques Offenbach, Giacomo Meyerbeer and Paul Dukas who were also of Jewish ancestry.

The stage doors of America soon opened to Jewish immigrants of musical genius. Popular culture hungered for musical theater, vaudeville and innovations in song derived from folk tunes, jazz and the gospel repertoire. Silent films were accompanied by offstage pianists, and newfangled "talkies" featured music from such early greats as Al Jolson.

Jewish song writers, lyricists, composers and performers soon became a dominant force in popular and classical music. Jerome Kern single-handedly invented the modern American musical. Irving Berlin laid early groundwork for the idiom of popular song. Straddling the classical and modern, the songs of George Gershwin became popular standards and much of the basis of jazz improvisation. And Aaron Copland and Leonard Bernstein produced striking symphonic works and scores for the theater and ballet.

American composers and instrumentalists of Jewish descent have influenced modern music performed worldwide. The clarinet of Benny Goodman, the vocal styles of Dinah Shore and Barbra

Streisand, and the lively patter songs of Danny Kaye have added their distinctive notes to jazz, pop and show tunes played everywhere.

Jewish immigrants have also excelled in interpreting and composing classical music. Russian-born violinists Jascha Heifetz, Mischa Elman and Nathan Milstein, and pianists Vladimir Horowitz and Arthur Rubinstein are stars in our musical firmament. Others from Germany and Austria include Rudolf Serkin, Arnold Schoenberg, Bruno Walter and Erich Leinsdorf.

From Bob Dylan to Isaac Stern, from Artie Shaw to George Szell, from Sophie Tucker to Richard Tucker, come the sounds of music heard around the world.

Composers of Popular, Jazz and Theater Music

HAROLD ARLEN (1905-86) b. Buffalo, NY
Songwriter In the opinion of many, he rivalled Irving Berlin and George Gershwin in the mastery of stage and film scores. His Oscar-winning "Over the Rainbow," "Stormy Weather" and "That Old Black Magic," endeared him to blues and pop audiences in the 1930s through 1950s. His top musicals include *Rythmania* (1931), *The Wizard of Oz* (1939) and *A Star is Born* (1954).

BURT BACHARACH (1928-) b. Kansas City, MO
Songwriter A 1968 Tony for the hit musical *Promises, Promises* was among numerous awards collected by a songwriter noted for melodic enchantment and polish. In long-time collaboration with lyricist Hal David, he earned an Oscar for an all-time favorite, "Raindrops Keep Falling on My Head." He also scored film music for *Butch Cassidy and the Sundance Kid* (1969) and *Arthur* (1982).

IRVING BERLIN (1888-1989) b. Temun, Russia
Songwriter The most productive songwriter in U.S. history laid a permanent foundation for popular American song. Among thirty

11

stage and seventeen film productions, and more than 3,000 tunes, are "Alexander's Ragtime Band," the hit that propelled him to fame, "I'm Dreaming of a White Christmas," "Easter Parade," and the country's unofficial national anthem, "God Bless America."

LEONARD BERNSTEIN (1918-90) b. Lawrence, MA
Composer/Conductor A legendary presence on the world's musical scene, he was hailed as music's most talented and articulate figure of his day. The gifted conductor, songwriter and composer of contemporary classics was equally noted as a pianist, author and popularizer of music via the national media. He is best remembered for his theatrical triumph *West Side Story* (1957).

JERRY BOCK (1928-) b. New Haven, CT
Composer His music helped *Fiorello!* (1959) win Broadway's triple crown: a Tony, Critics' Circle Award and Pulitzer Prize. Yet he is best known for *Fiddler on the Roof* (1964) which garnered nine Tonys and a measure of immortality. In frequent collaboration with lyricist Sheldon Harnick, he also wrote scores for *The Apple Tree* (1966) and *The Rothschilds* (1972).

CY COLEMAN (1929-) b. New York City
Composer/Pianist A prominent composer of his day, he received numerous awards and is remembered for a best song of the year Grammy nomination for "Witchcraft," in 1958. He has also collaborated with lyricists Dorothy Fields, Betty Comden and Adolph Green, and was nominated for a best musical Academy Award for *Sweet Charity* (1963).

NEIL DIAMOND (1941-) b. New York City
Composer/Singer His ardent and engaging vocal style, uniquely his from the first note, brought him to the forefront of the pop music

field with interpretations of country-rock, folk, ballad and gospel. Augmenting a busy schedule of concert tours, he composed and recorded music for two films: *Jonathan Livingston Seagull* and a remake of *The Jazz Singer* (1980).

BOB DYLAN (1941-) b. Duluth, MN
Composer/Singer With origins rooted in American folk tradition, his music and lyrics have richly inspired the changing voice of popular music. Evolving from folk to social protest songs, then to country-rock fusion, the body of his work shows daring innovation that continues to win the ear of large and loyal audiences around the world.

LEONARD FEATHER (1914-94) b. London, England
Jazz Critic The musician, composer and record producer was best known as a force for propagating classic jazz through his writings and tireless support of such greats as Duke Ellington, Count Basie and Louis Armstrong. The chronicler of jazz history authored *Inside Bebop* (1949), edited the *Encyclopedia of Jazz* and wrote an influential column for *The Los Angeles Times*.

GEORGE GERSHWIN (1898-1937) b. New York City
Composer His genius as a tunesmith was also mirrored in classical compositions in the jazz idiom. Stage scores for *Of Thee I Sing* (1932 Pulitzer) and *Porgy and Bess* (1935) were joined by the immortal *Rhapsody in Blue* (1923) and *An American in Paris* (1928). He bridged both forms with outstanding music featuring lyrics often written by his brother, Ira Gershwin (1896-1983).

ARLO GUTHRIE (1947-) b. New York City
Songwriter/Folksinger Influenced by his father, Woody, he launched a parallel career with his best known song, "Alice's

Restaurant" (1967), later adapted for a film in which he was cast. Throughout the 1960s and 1970s, he gained reputation as an exponent of country as well as folk music. He also mobilized resources to combat Huntington's Disease that felled his father.

MARVIN HAMLISCH (1944-) b. New York City

Composer/Pianist In adolescence he displayed great professional promise concertizing as a classical pianist. A career switch to composition in popular forms produced award-winning songs and musical adaptations for *The Sting* (1973), *The Way We Were* (1973) and *A Chorus Line* (1975). He simultaneously accepts piano engagements with symphony orchestras.

SYLVIA FINE KAYE (1913-91) b. New York City

Songwriter The spirited music and clever lyrics she wrote for her husband, Danny Kaye, sparkled in films like *The Secret Life of Walter Mitty* (1947), *The Inspector General* (1949) and *The Court Jester* (1956). Independent of their partnership, she won a Peabody Award for a public TV series *Musical Comedy Tonight* and an Emmy for children's TV programming in 1976.

JEROME KERN (1885-1945) b. New York City

Composer *Showboat* (1927) and *Roberta* (1933) were but two works by a prolific songwriter hailed as the father of the modern American musical. He transformed the operetta of his day into a new theatrical form graced with ageless sing-along melodies. His "Ol' Man River" and "Smoke Gets in Your Eyes" exemplify a lifetime repertoire of more than 1,000 songs.

FRANK LOESSER (1910-69) b. New York City

Composer/Lyricist The self-taught, multi-talented musician embraced the stage and motion pictures early in life, later earning kudos for making musical magic in *Guys and Dolls* (1950) and *Most Happy Fella* (1956). He wrote the words as well as music for the great majority of his ten productions. His signature tune, "Baby It's Cold Outside," is a lasting favorite.

FREDERICK LOEWE (1904-88) b. Berlin, Germany
Composer He wrote many of Broadway's most melodious and memorable songs. A 1942 meeting with lyricist Alan Jay Lerner began a collaboration producing such hits as *My Fair Lady* (1956), *Gigi* (1958) and *Camelot* (1960). Who will ever forget "You've Got a Hold on Me," "Almost Like Being in Love," "I Could Have Danced All Night" and "I Remember It Well?"

BARRY MANILOW (1946-) b. New York City
Songwriter/Singer His serene but infectious vocal style and out-pouring of songs have drawn sellout concerts and the reward of nearly a dozen platinum albums. The gentle balladeer at the keyboard also arranged the music that helped lift Bette Midler to stardom. Among his standout singles are "Mandy," "Could it be Magic," "This One's For You" and "Trying to Get the Feeling."

RICHARD RODGERS (1902-79) b. Hamels Station, NY
Composer He was a major figure in musical theater whose songs brightened shows including *Oklahoma!* (1943), *Carousel* (1945), *South Pacific* (1949), *The King and I* (1951) and *The Sound of Music* (1959) – among more than forty stage and film productions. He often teamed with lyricists Lorenz Hart and Oscar Hammerstein II, and scored the distinguished TV series, *Victory at Sea* (1952).

SIGMUND ROMBERG (1887-1951) b. Nagykanizsa, Hungary
Composer He emigrated to the U.S. in 1909 and wrote many romantic operettas and songs that bore echoes of his earlier Viennese influences. *The Student Prince* (1924), *The Desert Song* (1926) and *The New Moon* (1928) were among the more than seventy he composed. Included was notable music for *The Girl of the Golden West* and a legacy of over 2,000 popular songs.

HAROLD ROME (1908-93) b. Hartford, CT
Songwriter Satirical wit seasoned the large output of melodies written by a talent of deep social consciousness. His music and lyrics enriched such hits as *Pins and Needles* (1937), *Call Me Mister* (1946) and *I Can Get it for You Wholesale* (1962) which featured the Broadway debut of Barbra Streisand. He was elected to the Songwriters' Hall of Fame in 1981.

PAUL SIMON (1941-) b. Newark, NJ   *Songwriter/Singer*
ART GARFUNKLE (1941-) b. New York City   *Singer*
The folk rock music of these childhood friends entered the popular culture of the 1960s and 1970s – earning wider cross-generational appeal than the hard rock of the times. Simon composed many of their classics including "Sounds of Silence" and "Bridge Over Troubled Waters." They parted ways in the 1970s, but join occasionally for sellout concerts.

STEPHEN SONDHEIM (1930-) b. New York City
Composer/Lyricist He was lifted to the front ranks of musical theater by his lyrics for Leonard Bernstein's *West Side Story* (1957), and has since broken ground on his own frequently astonishing productions. His musical intelligence and economy, and sharp-witted and often cynical lyrics, are in top form in *A Little Night Music* (1973) and *Sweeney Todd* (1979).

16

JULE STYNE (1905-94) b. London, England
Songwriter Linked in melodic diction with Gershwin, Berlin, Rodgers and Porter, he composed scores of beguiling songs for stage and screen. They were written into his eighteen productions including *Anchors Aweigh* (1945), *It Happened in Brooklyn* (1947), *Gentlemen Prefer Blondes* (1949), *Bells Are Ringing* (1956), *Gypsy* (1959) and *Funny Girl* (1964).

KURT WEILL (1900-50) b. Dessau, Germany
Composer Although most closely associated with music for *The Three Penny Opera* (1928), he wrote other satirical operas and scores for *Knickerbocker Holiday* (1938) and *Street Scene* (1946). His bittersweet works with librettist Bertolt Brecht portray society shuttling between a sense of doom and allegiances to a gentler, happier past.

Lyricists

HOWARD ASHMAN (1951-91) b. Baltimore, MD
Lyricist/Playwright He helped bring several of Walt Disney's most bewitching films to the screen during a brief but productive life – sharing honors with composer Alan Menken for songs in *The Little Mermaid, Beauty and the Beast* and *Aladdin*. Their collaboration on the off-Broadway production of *The Little Shop of Horrors* (1982) won warm reviews.

OSCAR HAMMERSTEIN II (1895-1960) b. New York City
Lyricist Every person voicing a tune from the hit musicals *Oklahoma, Carousel, South Pacific, The Sound of Music, Show Boat* or a dozen others, applauds his stylish and memorable lyrics. He had collaborated with composers Jerome Kern, Sigmund Romberg and

Rudolph Friml before a 1943 partnership with Richard Rodgers which was more permanent and successful.

MARILYN BERGMAN   b. New York City
ALAN BERGMAN   b. New York City
Lyricists Through the years, the prolific husband and wife team received virtually every award presented by the film, theater and TV industries. In association with composers Marvin Hamlisch, Henry Mancini, Michel Legrand and others, they have written the lyrics for "The Windmills of Your Mind," and compelling film scores for *The Way We Were* and *A Star is Born*.

ADOLPH GREEN   (1915-)   b. New York City
Lyricist/Writer/Actor His long alliance with playwright Betty Comden gave Broadway and Hollywood decades of its most enduring, award-winning musicals: *Wonderful Town* (1953), *Bells are Ringing* (1960) and *The Will Rogers Follies* (1991) are among them. He spent his earliest years performing in nightclub and cabaret reviews, and is married to actress Phyllis Newman.

SHELDON HARNICK   (1924-)   b. Chicago, IL
Lyricist The former violinist began his theatrical career in the early 1950s by writing song lyrics for on and off-Broadway musical reviews. Later collaborations with Jerry Bock produced lyrics for the Tony and Pulitzer Prize-winning *Fiorello!* (1959), *Fiddler on the Roof* (1964) which won nine Tony awards, as well as for *A Christmas Carol* and *A Wonderful Life*.

ALAN JAY LERNER   (1918-85)   b. New York City
Lyricist No lyricist of the century has exceeded his count of musical hits on stage and screen. His chief successes in collaboration with composer Frederick Loewe included *Brigadoon* (1947),

My Fair Lady (1956), *Gigi* (1958) and *Camelot* (1960). The Harvard educated lyricist also produced an Oscar-winning book for *An American in Paris* (1951).

Other noted Songwriters and Composers

Edgar Harburg   Burton Lane

Alfred Newman   Phil Ochs

Arthur Schwartz   Arthur Siegel

Mike Stoller

Bandleaders, Musicians and Vocalists

EDDIE FISHER (1928-) b. Philadelphia, PA

Vocalist "Oh, My Papa" and "I'm in the Mood for Love" are familiar to a career studded with five gold records earned from 1951 to 1956. His vocals topped the charts between the reigns of the young Frank Sinatra and Elvis Presley. He was a celebrated TV show and night club performer with four Top Ten albums bought largely by teenagers and young adults.

STAN GETZ (1927-91) b. Philadelphia, PA

Jazz Musician The 15-year old prodigy on the saxophone rejected a scholarship to Julliard and joined the Jack Teagarden band. Months later, he played with Stan Kenton, perfecting his specialty, melodic improvisation. The jazz era found him in the reed sections of the Jimmy Dorsey, Benny Goodman and Woody Herman orchestras. His solos earned eleven Grammy awards.

BENNY GOODMAN (1909-86) b. Chicago, IL
Bandleader/Jazz Musician The "King of Swing" ushered in a new age of sophisticated jazz distinguished for its precision and purity. The brilliant jazz and classical clarinetist was at peak popularity from the mid-Thirties to the early Forties. Among other jazz greats once under his baton were Harry James, Teddy Wilson, Bunny Berigan, Lionel Hampton, Gene Krupa and Ziggy Elman.

STEVE LAWRENCE (1935-) b. New York City
EYDIE GORME (1932-) b. New York City
Vocalist Duo As a duo and singly, they have remained performing and recording artists since their 1957 marriage. Constantly on tour and on radio and TV, they have appeared in big name celebrity specials – opposite Bob Hope and Frank Sinatra in the past. Their four decades of song have been rewarded with the industry's most prestigious awards.

MITCH MILLER (1911-) b. Rochester, NY
Conductor/Producer The classically trained oboist moved to pop and jazz when he lifted the baton and cut his famed "Sing Along With Mitch" albums for Columbia and Mercury Records. He also staged a popular TV show which advanced the careers of vocalists Vic Damone and Tony Bennett. Occasionally he guest conducted orchestras in Europe and in the Americas.

ARTIE SHAW (1910-) b. New York City
Bandleader The jazz and swing big band leader played several instruments but made his mark as a clarinetist. He cut his first record in 1938, and scored and performed in several movies. Before retiring at the height of his career at age 44, he conducted a U.S. Navy band and the Gramercy 5 Chamber Ensemble. He was married to film stars Lana Turner and Ava Gardner.

DINAH SHORE (1917-94) b. Winchester, TN
Vocalist For more than thirty years, her radio and TV shows, recordings and film appearances were integral parts of the American scene. The entertainer was a G.I. favorite during World War Two. Pop songs like "Buttons and Bows" and "Love and Marriage" led her Hit Parade blockbusters. She also hosted a major women's golf pro tournament bearing her name.

MEL TORME (1925-) b. Chicago, IL
Vocalist Aptly called "The Velvet Fog," he headlined with top bands in the 1940s and 1950s, and his mellow, husky voice was heard on radio, in clubs, concert halls and over TV. His repertoire recently expanded to ballads and jazz, and has won listeners of all ages. The versatile crooner has also written songs and served as a musical advisor for TV specials.

SOPHIE TUCKER (1884-1966) b. Russia
Singer/Entertainer Her sentimental, effusive style took her from a small New York cafe in 1906 to a 1934 command performance before English royalty. In turn comic, brassy and raunchy, she starred in musicals, films and TV. The trademark tunes of "The Last of the Red Hot Mamas," as she was affectionately dubbed, were "My Yiddishe Momma," and "Some of These Days."

PAUL WHITEMAN (1891-1967) b. Denver, CO
Conductor The King of Jazz, as he was called, inaugurated symphonic jazz when he commissioned George Gershwin to compose and premiere *Rhapsody in Blue* in New York City's Aeolian Hall (1924). Bix Beiderbecke, Jack Teagarden and Jimmy Dorsey were among others who performed orchestral jazz under his direction. He also appeared in films and launched Bing Crosby's career.

Other Noted Bandleaders, Musicians and Vocalists

Larry Adler – harmonica virtuoso

Herb Alpert – founded Tijuana Brass

Nell Carter – singer

Leonard Cohen – singer/composer

Meyer Davis – bandleader

Eddie Duchin – bandleader

Cass Elliot – singer

Jack Elliot – singer

Ziggy Elman – trumpeter/bandleader

Helen Forrest – singer

Lesley Gore – singer/composer

Joel Grey – clarinetist/actor

Libby Holman – singer

Harry James – trumpeter/bandleader

Billy Joel – singer/composer

Mickey Katz – "Yiddish" jazz bandleader

Carole King – singer/composer

Lester Lanin – bandleader

Tony Martin – singer

Helen Reddy – singer

Neil Sedaka – singer/composer

Carly Simon – singer/composer

Composers of Classical and Modern Music

MARC BLITZSTEIN (1905-64) b. Philadelphia, PA
Composer While best remembered for his polished adaptation of
the Brecht/Weill *Threepenny Opera*, the composer-pianist contributed a large body of work with social content to the American
musical stage. His *Airborne Symphony* (1946) followed his service
in World War Two, as did incidental film music, the opera *Regina*
(1948) and the musical play *Reuben, Reuben* (1955).

ERNEST BLOCH (1880-1959) b. Geneva, Switzerland
Composer One of the more significant turn-of-the-century com-
·posers wrote dozens of orchestral and chamber works with Hebraic
overtones and universal appeal. Much of his music is neoclassical
with modern dissonances. He taught and composed abroad before
coming to America (1916) where he headed conservatories in
Cleveland and San Francisco (1920-30).

AARON COPLAND (1900-90) b. New York City
Composer His dramatic, melodious compositions, rich in jazz
and folksong elements, best represent the modern American school
of music which he helped create and nourish. The arresting "Copland sound" is captured in a half-dozen film scores, piano and
chamber music pieces, and in three outstanding ballets: *Billy the
Kid* (1938), *Rodeo* (1942) and *Appalachian Spring* (1944).

MORTON GOULD (1913-) b. New York City
Composer/Conductor The multi-faceted talent with a wide
range of compositional styles has written symphonies, chamber
music, film scores and ballets. He has also conducted radio and
concert hall orchestras in the U.S. and abroad. Many of his suites
and short pieces convey the resonances of American culture, as in
American Salute (1947) and *American Ballads* (1976).

PHILIP GLASS (1937-) b. Baltimore, MD
Composer Considered a minimalist, he is a foremost avant-garde composer whose work often captures the rhythmic beat of Indian ragas. With vision and daring, he composed several startling operatic compositions – *Einstein on the Beach* (1976), *Civil Wars* (1984) and *Hydrogen Jukebox* (1990) which have recruited a growing following among younger audiences.

ERICH KORNGOLD (1897-1957) b. Brunn, Austria-Hungary
Composer Millions of filmgoers in the 1930s and 1940s have heard his scores for *Anthony Adverse, Captain Blood, The Sea Hawk* and other screen gems of the period. Less well known was the body of chamber music and orchestral compositions admired by his peers, including Gustav Mahler, Richard Strauss and Giacomo Puccini.

ARNOLD SCHOENBERG (1874-1951) b. Vienna, Austria
Composer With his evolution of the 12-tone technique for organizing musical composition, he revolutionized modern music and almost single-handedly inspired a new classical form. The intellectually challenging, influential system structured dozens of his orchestral, stage, choral and chamber works which are increasingly performed and admired by concert goers.

WILLIAM SCHUMAN (1910-92) b. New York City
Composer During six decades of composition acclaimed for its craftsmanship, he wrote ten symphonies, five ballet scores, numerous chamber pieces and music for the stage and film. American jazz and folk song suffused his music which won Pulitzers in 1943 and 1985. He was president of the Julliard School of Music (1945-61) and the Lincoln Center for the Performing Arts.

Other Noted Classical and Modern Composers

Elmer Bernstein	David Diamond
Morton Feldman	Ernest Gold
Ted Harris	Frederick Jacobi
Leon Kirchner	Darius Milhaud
Oscar Straus	Dimitri Tiomkin
Franz Waxman	

Orchestra Conductors

ARTHUR FIEDLER (1894-1979) b. Boston, MA
Conductor He mounted the podium before the Boston Pops Orchestra in 1926 and shaped a finely tuned musical organization that became world famous through radio, recordings and television. He was much admired for his dignity and composure on stage, and was equally esteemed for his confident command of a repertoire of jazz, popular and classical music.

EDWIN FRANKO GOLDMAN (1878-1956) b. Louisville, KY
Conductor/Composer Many called him the American March King, a composer of more than 100 marches, and the bandmaster who introduced public outdoor concert programs in 1918. The former cornetist with the Metropolitan Opera Orchestra devoted his life to bringing new and old band music to the nation. He also authored standard texts on training and organizing bands.

OTTO KLEMPERER (1885-1973) b. Breslau, Germany
Conductor He was highly regarded for his interpretations of Mozart, Beethoven and Bruckner. In mid-career he established his musical base in America and conducted the Los Angeles Sym-

phony Orchestra from 1935-40. Despite disabling illnesses during many years on the podium, he valiantly concertized throughout the U.S., Germany, England and Israel.

ANDRE KOSTELANETZ (1901-80) b. Russia
Conductor Appreciation of serious music in America owes much to his popularization of semi-classical works on radio during and after the 1930s. The musical director of the CBS orchestra also cut numerous recordings and introduced the works of lesser-known composers to concert goers. During the 1970s, he was in great demand as a guest conductor for leading orchestras.

SERGE KOUSSEVITZKY (1874-1951) b. Vishni-Volotchok, Russia
Conductor The musical climate in our country was enriched by his cultivated performances of the early works of emerging composers such as George Gershwin and Aaron Copland. He led the Boston Symphony from 1924 to 1949 and raised its standing to world-class status. He also founded and performed at the renowned Berkshire Festival in Tanglewood, MA.

ERIC LEINSDORF (1912-93) b. Vienna, Austria
Conductor The maestro's superb musicianship was attributed to his sometimes overzealous emphasis on technique and precision. While a subject of controversy, his technical finesse brought him before some of the most renowned organizations in the world, including the Metropolitan Opera Orchestra (1937), the Cleveland Orchestra and the Boston Symphony.

JAMES LEVINE (1943-) b. Cincinnati, OH
Conductor He conducted the Metropolitan Opera Orchestra since 1974 and assumed the opera company's artistic direction a decade later. His control of all aspects of operatic production helped create

an excellent musical organization. During furloughs from the Met he led the Chicago Symphony and Vienna Philharmonic, among others, and he has recorded extensively.

EUGENE ORMANDY (1899-1985) b. Budapest, Hungary
Conductor Under his direction from 1938 to 1980, the Philadelphia Orchestra developed a singular musical style that was richly colorful and romantic: the virtuoso "Philadelphia sound." He had performed as a solo violinist in early career, and was appointed to his first conducting post with the Minneapolis Symphony Orchestra in 1931.

ANDRE PREVIN (1929-) b. Berlin, Germany
Conductor/Composer A musician of many dimensions, he conducted major orchestras in the U.S. and Europe, scored music for stage and screen, and has written chamber and piano pieces. The four-time Oscar winner also recorded a series of successful jazz piano albums, and was musical director of the Los Angeles Philharmonic Orchestra and Royal Philharmonic Orchestra of London.

ARTUR RODZINSKI (1894-1958) b. Spalato, Dalmatia
Conductor He was credited by the music world as the finest molder of orchestras of his day. After leaving his mark on the Philadelphia Orchestra and Los Angeles Philharmonic, he forged the Cleveland Orchestra into an organization of international repute (1933-43). The NBC Orchestra, New York Philharmonic and Chicago Orchestra also flourished under his baton.

GEORGE SOLTI (1912-) b. Budapest, Hungary
Conductor He is best known for his mastery of the operatic medium, expressly his dynamic interpretations of Wagner. He directed the famed Covent Garden Opera in London from 1961 to

1971. Overlapping commitments on two continents added to his stature as leader of the Chicago Symphony (1969-89) and the London Philharmonic (1979-83).

MICHAEL TILSON THOMAS (1944-) b. Los Angeles, CA
Conductor Respect for his musical intuition brought him before the Boston, Los Angeles, Buffalo, Cleveland and London symphony orchestras. Eclectic in tastes, he has conducted and recorded European romantics and American moderns with a vivacity that has earned international awards. He also organized Florida's youth orchestra, the New World Symphony.

BRUNO WALTER (1876-1962) b. Berlin, Germany
Conductor He gained prominence as a musical director in Germany and Austria before Nazi oppression drove him to the U.S. From his adopted podium, he led the Metropolitan Opera, NBC Symphony and New World Philharmonic. A conductor in the romantic tradition, he built a large reputation on recordings of Beethoven, Brahms, Mahler and Bruckner.

Other Noted Orchestra Conductors

Maurice Abravanel	**Misha Dichter**
Antal Dorati	**Fritz Reiner**
Julius Rudel	**Max Rudolf**
George Szell	**Alfred Wallenstein**

Instrumentalists

MISCHA ELMAN (1891-1967) b. Talnoye, Russia
Violinist He first concertized at age eight and within five years began touring the stages of Berlin, London and New York. Regarded by some as a virtuoso of Jascha Heifetz's caliber, he differed from him in the lushness and resonance of what became known as "the Elman tone." He cut many albums and composed songs and pieces for his instrument.

JASCHA HEIFETZ (1901-87) b. Vilna, Lithuania
Violinist The child prodigy matured into an artist whose virtuosity combined reasoned interpretation and technical mastery. He was often described as the finest violinist of his time, having achieved a unique level of classical and romantic perfection. The musician also brought many works of emerging composers to America's concert halls.

VLADIMIR HOROWITZ (1904-89) b. Kiev, Russia
Pianist It is widely held that his technical brilliance and power within the romantic repertoire were unsurpassed by pianists of his generation. He concertized throughout the world until retirement in 1953, and made stunning returns before White House and Moscow audiences in 1967. He was married to the daughter of conductor Arturo Toscanini.

WANDA LANDOWSKA (1879-1959) b. Warsaw, Poland
Harpsichordist/Pianist The greatest harpsichordist of the century received her musical training in Berlin during the 1890s. Her artistry revived interest in the instrument and its work. She toured widely on the Continent and made her American debut with the Philadelphia Orchestra. The founder of the School of Ancient Music in Paris made her home in the U.S. since 1941.

YEHUDI MENUHIN   (1916-)   b. New York City
Violinist/Conductor Among the world's foremost musicians, he appeared in concert at age eight and performed as a soloist and conductor with leading symphony orchestras for more than a half century. He toured and recorded extensively throughout his career and organized several prestigious music festivals in England and Switzerland.

NATHAN MILSTEIN   (1904-92)   b. Odessa, Russia
Violinist/Composer A friendship with pianist Vladimir Horowitz opened doors that brought his talent to the world. He concertized in Europe, the U.S. and Canada after emigrating to the West in the 1920s. He was a composer and arranger as well, and his elegant style, purity of tone and unerring technique were undiminished as he performed into his eighties.

MURRAY PERAHIA   (1947-)   b. New York City
Pianist/Conductor He is regarded one of today's finest interpreters of romantic music, particularly of Chopin, Schumann and Mendelssohn. Since achieving fame by capturing the prestigious Leeds Festival Prize in 1972, he has concertized widely with major symphony orchestras and plays recitals with chamber ensembles, several of which he also conducts.

ITZHAK PERLMAN   (1945-)   b. Tel Aviv, Israel
Violinist Dazzling technique and melodic warmth have placed him among world-class violinists since the 1960s. He made his concert debut at age ten, six years after being disabled by polio. His first U.S. appearance at Carnegie Hall in 1963 was followed by performances with the New York Philharmonic and before worldwide audiences.

ARTHUR RUBINSTEIN (1887-1982) b. Vikhvatinetz, Russia
Pianist Music critics and international audiences hailed him as the Twentieth Century's most radiant and memorable player of the modern romantic repertoire. His lyrical, poetic and lucent perform-ances often featured the music of Chopin, as well as less well known Spanish works in first major performance. He typically scheduled one-hundred or more concerts annually.

ARTUR SCHNABEL (1882-1951) b. Lipnik, Moravia
Pianist/Composer In his time he was accepted as a foremost interpreter of Beethoven, Mozart and Schubert, who first won notice in Europe for his seamless performances. A chamber musi-cian, as well, he arrived in the U.S. in 1939, toured the nation's leading concert halls and composed orchestral pieces. His three symphonies touched on the boundaries of modernism.

RUDOLF SERKIN (1903-91) b. Bohemia
Pianist His musical gifts as a child were fostered by family and professional musicians. He soloed with the Vienna Symphony at age four. Best known for his Bach and Mozart, he also brought his musicianship to chamber music, accompanied by his father-in-law, violinist Adolf Busch. He headed Philadelphia's Curtis Institute of Music from 1968 to 1978.

ISAAC STERN (1920-) b. Kremenets, Russia
Violinist An illustrious musical career was launched in 1936 at his first performance with the San Francisco Symphony. He was principally associated with the New York Philharmonic, and he earned critical acclaim for his dramatic renderings of orchestral and chamber works. His strong support underwrote a protest movement that saved New York's Carnegie Hall from demolition.

PINCHAS ZUCKERMAN (1948-) b. Tel Aviv, Israel
Violinist/Conductor The protégé of Isaac Stern studied at Julliard and launched his career after winning a Leventritt Competition prize in 1967. A violinist of refinement and authority, he is also a violist and conductor, and has led chamber ensembles and major orchestras including the New York Philharmonic and Boston Symphony. He is married to actress Tuesday Weld.

Other Noted Instrumentalists

Emanuel Ax – pianist

Alexander Brailowsky – pianist

Emanuel Feuermann – cellist

Boris Goldovsky – pianist/conductor

Gary Graffman – pianist

William Kappel – pianist

Gregor Piatigorsky – cellist

Leonard Rose – cellist

Rosalyn Tureck – pianist

Efram Zimbalist – violinist

Paul Zukofsky – violinist

Opera Singers

ROBERT MERRILL (1919-) b. New York City
Baritone His early plans for a baseball career yielded to a future on stage for his resonant and flexible voice of dramatic intensity. Diligent study earned him a Metropolitan Opera debut in 1945, and numerous appearances on radio. The much admired and

popular star excelled in Italian and French opera during his long association with the Met.

JAN PEERCE (1904-84) b. New York City
Tenor "The Bluebird of Happiness" became a vocal logo of the limpid voice heard in the 1930s over the nationally beamed Radio City Music Hall of the Air. Arturo Toscanini redirected him to the dramatic stage on which he sang leading roles at the Metropolitan Opera for more than a generation. Concurrently he was in high demand as a cantor and TV guest.

ROBERTA PETERS (1930-) b. New York City
Coloratura The twenty-year old artist made her dramatic Metropolitan Opera debut standing in for an ailing prima donna in *Don Giovanni*. She has since performed on the Met stage for a record-breaking three decades, and had enjoyed many encore appearances on the *Ed Sullivan Show*. The coloratura sang her most notable roles in *La Traviata* and *La Boheme*.

REGINA RESNIK (1922-) b. New York City
Mezzo-soprano The star of New York's Metropolitan Opera was equally admired on European tours for her passionate musical performances. Several leads among the approximately eighty roles she sung are quintessentially hers – in Bizet's *Carmen*, Tchaikovsky's *Queen of Spades*, Verdi's *Falstaff* and Strauss's *Elektra*. She has also acted in legitimate theater.

BEVERLY SILLS (1929-) b. New York City
Coloratura-soprano A shining presence on stage for more than thirty years, she conquered music critics and audiences with her poise, charm and exquisite tone. The diva with the New York City Opera from 1955 to 1980 made her first appearance with the

Metropolitan Opera in 1975. Retired as a performer, she is currently the managing director of the New York City Opera.

RISE STEVENS (1913-) b. New York City
Soprano Her 1938 debut with the New York Metropolitan Opera launched a romance with an international following which was as impressed with her acting as with her pure lyric soprano voice. Appearing in films and on her own radio show (1945), she was revered for title roles in *Der Rosenkavalier*, *The Marriage of Figaro* and for her ardent, tragic *Carmen*.

RICHARD TUCKER (1913-75) b. New York City
Tenor The singer began his career as a cantor, and at age 32 won coast-to-coast fame on radio's Chicago Theater of the Air. A triumphant debut at the Metropolitan Opera soon followed, and he became known as a leading lyric tenor in Italian and French opera. His critically successful appearances, worldwide, earned him the title of America's Caruso.

Other Noted Opera Singers

Alma Gluck   Alexander Kipnis
Evelyn Lear   Judith Raskin
Friedreich Schorr   Jennie Tourel
Leonard Warren

Musical Entrepreneurs

OSCAR HAMMERSTEIN I (1847-1919) b. Berlin, Germany
Impresario The member of a family of musical entrepreneurs was best known as the builder of ten American opera houses and theaters to which he brought numerous singers and productions. Among his properties were the Harlem Opera House (1888) and the Manhattan Opera House (1906). He was dedicated to popularizing grand opera, and was also a respected journalist and composer.

DAVID MANNES (1866-1959) b. New York City
Musicologist/Educator The violinist who joined the New York Symphony in 1891 left twenty years later to establish a first of its kind: a music school for gifted black youngsters. Within four years he founded the David Mannes School of Music which was accredited as a college in 1953. The institution continues to graduate some of the foremost American and foreign-born musicians.

Three
Literature, Arts and Architecture

By the 6th Century B.C.E., Jewish scholars and scribes had unified what is today called the Books of the Bible. Their pages glowed with the beauty of the Psalms, Song of Songs, the Lamentations and Koheleth which glorified the divine purpose of the supreme being. These writings constituted a prized literature close to the hearts and souls of devout Jews.

Not until the 18th and 19th Centuries did Jewish secular literature emerge in Eastern Europe. Written almost entirely in Hebrew or Yiddish, the works had small audiences outside of Jewish communities.

When in America, immigrants were no longer confined to intellectual ghettos. Freedom of expression prompted literary expansion. Yiddish rapidly gave way to English as the language of choice of "progressive" Jewish writers and readers. What's more, federal legislation in 1906 and 1913 obliged immigrants to pass literacy tests for entry, an inducement for millions of foreigners to learn to read and write in the tongue of their adopted homeland.

Many newly-arrived Jews with literary inclinations discovered fertile soil for growth – earlier tilled by scholars such as Mayer Sulzberger, an erudite man of letters who chaired the American Jewish Committee at its founding in 1906. His organization, allied with the Jewish Publication Society of America (organized in 1888) and the Central Conference of American Rabbis (dating from 1889), urged and sponsored English instruction.

American readers are also indebted to renowned Jewish-European authors: Franz Kafka, Rainer Maria Rilke, Franz Werfel, Heinrich Heine, Ferenc Molnar, André Maurois, Boris Pasternak and others. But the list is short in contrast with Jewish-American writers of this century: fiction writers, essayists, poets, dramatists and critics. Edna Ferber, Dorothy Parker, Gertrude

Stein, Irwin Shaw, Norman Mailer, Herman Wouk, Joseph Heller, Philip Roth and Nobel Prize winners Saul Bellow, I.B. Singer and Joseph Brodsky, to name a few.

The fine arts in America were also inspired by European greats of Jewish origin: Amedeo Modigliani, Chaim Soutine, Marc Chagall and Camille Pissarro, a founder of the French impressionist movement. Baron Joseph Duveen, perhaps the world's preeminent art dealer of his day, acquired priceless collections of European masters for the estates and mansions of English and American clients.

Our native Jewish painters and sculptors of the 20th Century belong to all schools of the creative arts. Ben Shawn, Max Weber, Jack Levine, Raphael Soyer, Jo Davidson, Chaim Gross, Louise Nevelson, Mark Rothko and George Segal are among the best known.

They prospered in the intoxicating air of freedom of expression, our nation's birthright.

Authors and Poets

ISAAC ASIMOV (1920-92) b. Petrovichi, Russia

Author/Biochemist He was among the most prolific writers of his day, authoring and editing more than 475 books on science, religion, literature and history. A simultaneous master of science fiction, he is best known for *I Robot* (1950) and *The Foundation Trilogy* (1951-52), and for introductions to science including *The Intelligent Man's Guide to Science* (1960).

SAUL BELLOW (1915-) b. Lachine, Canada

Novelist The acknowledged dean of contemporary American novelists won a Pulitzer Prize in 1975 for *Humbolt's Gift* and a Nobel Prize for Literature the following year. A short story writer and playwright as well, he received three National Book Awards. His notable works include *The Adventures of Augie March* (1953), *Herzog* (1964) and *Mr. Sammler's Planet* (1970).

37

JOSEPH BRODSKY (1940-) b. St. Petersburg, Russia
Poet His biting, ironic verse was suppressed by the Soviets who imprisoned him as a "social parasite." Russian countrymen knew only of the fluent linguist's translations. After emigrating to the U.S. in 1972, he openly published political poetry of a high order. The winner of a Nobel Prize for Literature in 1987 served as America's fifth Poet Laureate in 1991.

E.L. DOCTOROW (1931-) b. New York City
Novelist His fiction is intriguingly rooted in the factual world and speaks to the hopes and fears of ordinary people and celebrities, of those ennobled by fate and circumstance. Literary fame came with *Welcome to Hard Times* (1961). *Ragtime* (1975), a fiercely nostalgic look at the turbulent years following the turn of the century, was filmed in 1981.

JASON EPSTEIN (1928-) b. Cambridge, MA
Author/Editor/Publisher Leaving a vice presidency at Random House, he joined Doubleday & Company (1951-58) as chief editor for Philip Roth, Gore Vidal, W.H. Auden and others. He founded *The New York Review of Books* (1963), later wrote *The Great Conspiracy Trial of Random House,* and was the first to receive a National Book Award Medal for distinguished contributions to American letters (1988).

HOWARD FAST (1914-) b. New York City
Novelist His biographical and historical novels received wide attention in the Forties and Fifties. The author's sympathies for social and political justice prevail in such respected works as *The Last Frontier* (1942), *Citizen Tom Paine* (1943) and *Sparticus* (1952). Initially a leftist writer, he renounced Communism in his harshly critical *The Naked God* (1957).

EDNA FERBER (1887-1968) b. Kalamazoo, MI
Novelist/Playwright The landscape of America and the interior lives of its people inspired the Pulitzer Prize-winning *So Big* (1924). Other classics of their genre like *Show Boat* (1926) were adapted for musicals. Her novels also include *Giant* (1952) and *Ice Palace* (1958). *Dinner at Eight* (1932) and *Stage Door* (1936) were written for the theater with collaborator George S. Kaufman.

BRUCE JAY FRIEDMAN (1930-) b. New York City
Novelist/Playwright He emerged in the 1960s with a group of influential writers, including Salinger and Roth, as chroniclers of the Jewish experience in America. From that perspective he authored the critical success *Stern* (1962) and the funny and touching *Mother's Kisses* (1963). Among his other writings are the plays *Scuba Duba* (1967) and *Steambath* (1970).

ALLEN GINSBERG (1926-) b. Newark, NJ
Poet He may be the most widely read contemporary American poet, here and around the world. In musical and muscular stanzas sounding the message of the Beat Generation, his major work was reflective of Zen Buddhism and as visionary as that of Walt Whitman. His epic poems include *Howl* (1956), an incisive look at American Society, and *Kaddish* (1961), a lament to his mother's death.

JAMES GOLDMAN (1927-) b. Chicago, IL
Novelist/Screenwriter He is best known for the novel *Waldorf* (1965) and for the Oscar-winning screenplay *Lion in Winter* (1967). His other writings include the novels *Myself as Witness* (1980), *Fulton County* (1989) and screenplays for *Nicholas & Alexandra* (1971) and *Robin and Marian* (1976). His semi-documentary *Anastasia* appeared on TV in 1986.

DAVID HALBERSTAM (1934-) b. New York City
Author/Journalist The globe-trotting *New York Times* reporter covered beats in The Congo and Poland, then in Vietnam from which he filed perceptive pieces that later entered his Pulitzer Prize-winning work *The Best and the Brightest* (1972). Among his thirteen other books are *The Reckoning* (1972), a history of the Nissan and Ford auto companies, and *Summer of '49* (1990), a tribute to American baseball.

JOSEPH HELLER (1923-) b. New York City
Novelist Following service in the U.S. Army Air Force during World War Two, he produced a satirical novel about the military, *Catch 22* (1961), a bestseller whose title entered the language as a "winless dilemma." The play *We Bombed in New Haven* (1968) and his novels *Something Happened* (1974), *Good as Gold* (1979) and *God Knows* (1984) secure his literary reputation.

FANNIE HURST (1889-1968) b. Hamilton, OH
Novelist In addition to a productive and successful literary career, the author of *Stardust* (1921) and *Back Street* (1930) helped support many social and civic causes including the New York Urban League. She was also an active and outspoken crusader for women's rights and a patron of the arts. Much of her work was adapted for films and is also in foreign translation.

ERICA JONG (1942-) b. New York City
Novelist/Poet Her erotic novels often convey sexually liberating messages for contemporary women. She appeared on the literary scene with *Fear of Flying* (1973) and recently published *Fear of Fifty* (1994). Also a talented poet, she has taught at major universities and has been accorded the 1963 American Academy of Poets Award among other honors.

JERZY KOSINSKI (1933-91) b. Lodz, Poland
Novelist An intensity of conviction and bizarre episodes of violence gave brutal impact to his novels of survival. His early experiences in his native country were as wrenching as some described in his books. *The Painted Bird* (1965) captured the Holocaust in its shattering particulars, and the equally arresting *Steps* won a National Book Award in 1969.

JUDITH KRANTZ (1927-) b. New York City
Novelist Her novel *Scruples*, issued in the late 1970s, clung to the bestseller list for a year. The former publicist and fashion editor sustained her quick literary rise with a number of sequels. Among her painstakingly researched novels with complex and engrossing plots was *Princess Daisy* (1983), one of several adapted for TV mini-series.

STANLEY KUNITZ (1905-) b. Worcester, MA
Poet/Educator He composed meticulously crafted poetry while teaching at leading universities since 1946. *Selected Poems, 1928 to 1958* won a Pulitzer Prize in 1958. His mostly formal poetry gradually increased in vision, as represented in his hallmark collection *The Testing Tree* (1971). He also served as a poetry consultant to the U.S. Library of Congress.

IRA LEVIN (1929-) b. New York City
Novelist/Playwright His novels *A Kiss Before Dying* (1953) and *Rosemary's Baby* (1967) were chilling forerunners of his now classic *The Stepford Wives* (1972). Many of his works were adapted for film. A playwright, as well, he has written *No Time for Sergeants* (1955) and *Death Trap* (1978), one of Broadway's record-breaking long-running shows.

MEYER LEVIN (1906-81) b. Chicago, IL
Novelist/Screenwriter *Compulsion* (1956) was a bestseller that gained national recognition for the dramatist, screenwriter and former news correspondent. An earlier novel *The Old Bunch* (1937) was praised for its perceptive realism, a quality that also characterized his documentary films, most typically *The Illegals* produced in 1977.

NORMAN MAILER (1923-) b. Long Branch, NJ
Novelist His first novel *The Naked and the Dead* (1948) was the tour de force that established him as a major literary newcomer at age 25. He pursues his passionate involvement with social and political issues, and is recognized as an outstanding if often pugnacious and controversial journalist. *The Armies of the Night* (1969) and *The Executioner's Song* (1980) won Pulitzer Prizes.

BERNARD MALAMUD (1914-86) b. New York City
Novelist People at risk or in moral dilemma define his short stories and novels – characters he described as "simple people struggling to make their lives better in a world of bad luck." His critically acclaimed works, which earned a Pulitzer Prize and two National Book Awards, include *The Natural* (1952), *The Assistant* (1957), *The Magic Barrel* (1958) and *The Fixer* (1966).

HOWARD NEMEROV (1920-91) b. New York City
Poet/Essayist America's Poet Laureate from 1988 to 1990 was a distinguished educator, scholar and a poet of delicate insight and a keen sense of the times. Some of his work was inspired by his experiences during World War Two and by the nation's space program. *The Collected Poems of Howard Nemerov* received a Pulitzer Prize and a National Book Award in 1961.

CYNTHIA OZICK   (1928-)   b. New York City
Author/Literary Critic   Following publication of her first book *Trust* (1966), her novels, short stories and essays have been praised by peers and critics for their scrupulous craftsmanship and intellectual vigor. Her writings have dealt with mysticism, Judaic history and philosophy, and are conspicuous for their humor, insightfulness and integrity.

DOROTHY PARKER   (1893-1967)   b. West End, NJ
Author/Poet   She was noted for her bitter wit, spare verse and her satirical short stories which appeared regularly in *The New Yorker*. With Robert Benchley, the part-time playwright and screenwriter co-founded the famed Algonquin (Hotel) Round Table which drew literary luminaries. Her works included *Laments for the Living* (1930), *Death and Taxes* (1931) and *Here Lies* (1939).

S.J. PERELMAN   (1904-79)   b. New York City
Author/Humorist   The linguistic acrobatics of the fertile punster delighted readers of his *New Yorker* magazine stories. He also wrote scripts for Hollywood comedies, including several for the Marx Brothers. His impish wit and mockery of conventions appeared in collections including *Strictly from Hunger* (1937), *The Rising Gorge* (1961) and *Vinegar Puss* (1975).

AYN RAND   (1905-82)   b. St. Petersburg, Russia
Novelist/Philosopher   Several controversial novels espoused her philosophy of objectivism, proposing "rational selfishness" as a proper impulse behind living the moral life while achieving happiness. *The Fountainhead* (1943), which she later adapted as a screen play, and *Atlas Shrugged* (1957) dramatized her theories which still attract a following.

HAROLD ROBBINS (1916-) b. New York City
Novelist Astronomical U.S. book sales and translations published in 63 countries rank him among the most widely read authors of modern times. His contemporary stories resonate with sexy and charismatic characters. *Never Love a Stranger* (1948), *The Carpetbaggers* (1961), which enjoyed seventy printings, and other novels were adapted for TV and films.

LEO ROSTEN (1908-) b. Lodz, Poland
Novelist/Political Scientist His early novel *The Education of H*Y*M*A*N   K*A*P*L*A*N* (1937), written under the pen name, Leonard Q. Ross, overshadowed his primary career as a distinguished government analyst and consultant. He also "moonlighted" screenplays, anthologies of humor, essays and the novel *Captain Newman, M.D.* (1962) which was later scripted for a motion picture.

PHILIP ROTH (1933-) b. Newark, NJ
Novelist The wry chronicler of the lives of people struggling for self-actualization gained early recognition for *Goodbye, Columbus*, a 1960 National Book Award winner. Scores of short stories and novels followed, including *Portnoy's Complaint* (1969), *My Life as a Man* (1974), *Zuckerman Unbound* (1981) and *Deceptions* (1990). He is wedded to Jewish actress Claire Bloom.

J. D. SALINGER (1919-) b. New York City
Novelist His first novel *Catcher in the Rye* (1951) won critical favor and the attention of young adult readers who identified with the image and adventures of its hero, Holden Caulfield. He subsequently published short stories in leading magazines, many featuring his literary invention, the Glass family. A second bestseller *Franny and Zooey* appeared in 1961.

BUDD SCHULBERG   (1914-)   b. New York City
Novelist   The spiritual penalties of a pitiless drive for fame and power often animate his stories, as in his signature work *What Makes Sammy Run?* (1941). Others include *The Harder They Fall* (1947), *The Disenchanted* (1950), based on F. Scott Fitzgerald's life story, and *Some Faces in the Crowd* (1953). He also scripted the Oscar-winning *On the Waterfront* in 1955.

MAURICE SENDAK   (1928-)   b. New York City
Author/Illustrator   Several generations of American children have grown up with the magical creatures of fantasy and mischief in his triumphal *Where the Wild Things Are* (1963) and in its many sequels. The nation's best known creator of children's books has also directed children's theater, taught at Yale University and has written lyrics for TV specials.

IRWIN SHAW   (1913-1984)   b. New York City
Novelist/Playwright   The images of World War Two, in which he served, were often metaphors in his novels and plays for the cruelties imposed on innocents by social systems and conventions. Typical were *The Young Lions* (1948), an outstanding first novel, and plays including *Bury the Dead* (1936) and *Sons and Soldiers* (1944). He was also engaged in writing for TV.

ISAAC BASHEVIS SINGER   (1904-91)   b. Radzymin, Poland
Novelist   Much of his earlier works recaptured the buoyant, sensual world of Jewish village life in Eastern Europe. Since arriving in America (1935), the teller of tales written in Yiddish often wove fantasy and mysticism into novels and short stories with contemporary settings. A 1974 National Book Award for *A Crown of Feathers* was followed by a Nobel Prize for Literature in 1978.

GERTRUDE STEIN (1874-1946) b. Pittsburgh, PA
Author The influential writer, critic and patron of the arts moved to Paris in 1903, gathering around her such disciples in early career like Sherwood Anderson, F. Scott Fitzgerald and Ernest Hemingway. Pablo Picasso and Paul Cezanne also befriended the literary innovator who created a personal language in *Three Lives* (1909) and *The Making of Americans* (1925).

IRVING STONE (1903-89) b. San Francisco, CA
Novelist The master of the biographical novel combined factual and fictional narrative in recounting the private lives of the famous. He featured Vincent Van Gōgh in *Lust for Life* (1934), Michelangelo in *The Agony and the Ecstacy* (1961) and Charles Darwin in *The Origin* (1980). Camille Pissarro, Jack London and Eugene Debs were also subjects of his novels.

LEON URIS (1924-) b. Baltimore, MD
Novelist Millions have read the riveting works of the U.S. Marine who launched his literary career with *Battle Cry* (1953), a highly praised war novel. *Exodus* (1957) was among the most popular American works of fiction ever written. Other bestsellers include *Topaz* (1967), *QB VII* (1970) and *Trinity* (1976). Several were successfully adapted for the screen.

IRVING WALLACE (1916-90) b. Chicago, IL
Novelist Years in journalism gave authenticity and credibility to his plots and characters. In *The Word* (1972), his fictional account of the discovery of a new gospel was taken as fact by many readers persuaded by his exhaustively researched material. *The Chapman Report* (1960) and *The Prize* (1962) were among his bestsellers that attracted an estimated 600 million readers.

NATHANIEL WEST (1903-40) b. New York City
Novelist/Screenwriter His four novellas, rich in fantasy, earned the praise of reviewers and readers largely after his premature death. He had been associated with the surrealistic writers movement before authoring his best known work *Miss Lonelyhearts* (1933) which he also adapted for the screen. Other works include *A Cool Million* (1934) and *The Day of the Locust* (1939).

ELIE WIESEL (1928-) b. Sighet, Romania
Novelist The chronicler of the Holocaust earned a Nobel Prize for Peace in 1986 for his inquiry into the moral and spiritual implications of the European calamity. More than a score of influential books by the Auschwitz survivor include *Jews of Silence* (1966) and *Souls on Fire* (1972). He is also a global lecturer and missionary for understanding and tolerance.

HERMAN WOUK (1915-) b. New York City
Novelist His psychological novel of World War Two, *The Caine Mutiny* (1951), won a Pulitzer Prize in 1952 and was adapted for stage and film. Within the same thematic framework, he wrote *The Winds of War* (1971) and *War and Remembrance* (1978), novels serialized on TV and seen by millions. *Marjorie Morningstar* (1955) and *Youngblood Hawke* were also made into films.

Other Noted Authors and Poets

Sholem Asch	**Maxwell Bodenheim**
Edward Dahlberg	**Babette Deutsch**
Stanley Elkin	**Herbert Gold**
Albert Halper	**Kenneth Koch**

Maxine Kumin	Annie Leibowitz
Denise Levertov	Philip Levine
Martin Mayer	Robert Nathan
Grace Paley	Marge Piercy
Chaim Potok	Jerome Weidman
Adrienne Rich	M.L. Rosenthal
Henry Roth	Muriel Rukeyser
Eric Segal	Susan Fromberg Schaeffer
Delmore Schwartz	Karl Shapiro
Harvey Shapiro	Sidney Sheldon
Gerald Stern	Ida Tarbell
Theodore Weiss	

Artists and Sculptors

BERNARD BERENSON (1865-1959) b. Vilnius, Lithuania
Art Critic Although educated in America, he lived most of his life in Italy from where his influence as an art historian extended worldwide. His counsel was sought by wealthy collectors who retained him to purchase modern and historic works of art. While some of his writings were controversial, many books including *Italian Painters of the Renaissance* (1894) remain classics.

JO DAVIDSON (1883-1952) b. New York City
Sculptor The visual power of his stone portraits of General Pershing, Woodrow Wilson, Franklin D. Roosevelt and Albert Einstein owes a debt to his inspiration, Auguste Rodin. He distilled the personalities of his subjects into sculptures that earned him world attention. His best known legacy is a huge Walt Whitman bronze in Palisades Interstate Park, NY.

48

CLEMENT GREENBERG (1909-94) b. New York City
Art Critic With authority and conviction he helped bring the art world a new and powerful art form: abstract expressionism. Beginning in the late Thirties, the medium's most articulate exponent championed the paintings of Jackson Pollock which personified the movement. His writings and lectures on art theory are classics of style and clarity.

CHAIM GROSS (1904-91) b. Wolow, Poland
Sculptor Female acrobats and mothers playing with children were frequent subjects for the master carver in wood and stone. He rose rapidly in the art world with arresting expressionistic forms including his epochal "Strong Woman" (1935). A gifted teacher, lecturer and writer, he presented his theories on sculptural craft in *The Techniques of Wood Sculpture* (1957).

LEE KRASNER (1908-84) b. New York City
Artist She was an abstract expressionist of high order and a force in the New York art scene for more than forty years. Her constantly evolving styles and inventive use of color and form projected intensity and ferocity seldom before seen in the works of female painters. The wife of artist Jackson Pollack was widely admired for her uniformly powerful canvases.

JACK LEVINE (1915-) b. Boston, MA
Artist A strong sense of social justice invested his work as a war artist in World War Two and later as a witness to the seamier elements of American life. The subjects of his often macabre conceptions are as diverse as J.P. Morgan, common laborers and Old Testament figures. Meticulous craftsmanship and vivid, raw colors give immediacy and command to his messages.

ROY LICHTENSTEIN (1923-) b. New York City
Artist He temporarily retired from abstract expressionism in the early 1960s and went on to win recognition for oversized recreations of comic book figures. The early visionary of the pop art school continues to evolve other forms and styles on the frontiers of modernism. His canvases are widely exhibited in prominent galleries and have appeared in major retrospectives.

JACQUES LIPCHITZ (1891-1973) b. Druskininkai, Lithuania
Sculptor The pioneering exponent of cubist sculpture shaped abstractions from spindly, delicate forms during his earliest period – typically, *Man with a Guitar* and *Bather* (1916). His work during and after the Twenties, including *The Spirit of Enterprise* and his famous *Figure*, marked a turn to larger scale, sensuality and bulky clay constructions shaped under water.

MAN RAY (1890-1976) Philadelphia, PA
Artist/Photographer The trailblazing painter and photographer was in the vanguard of the dadaist movement in New York. He developed the "Rayograph," a method of reproducing photographic prints in the darkroom, bypassing the camera. While living and working in France, he also produced several surrealistic films with Marcel Duchamp, notably *Anemic Cinema* (1924).

LARRY RIVERS (1925-) b. New York City
Artist His "Washington Crossing the Delaware" (1953) marked his own crossing from abstract expressionism to new forms which merged representational and abstract art. Ahead of their time, his canvases predated the pop art era and the post-modernist school. He was also the first American artist to populate paintings with commonplace devices like product logos and street posters.

MARK ROTHKO (1903-70) b. Dvinsk, Russia
Artist The works of one of America's most persuasive painters pay homage to abstract expressionism, surrealism and cubism. He was an evolving force behind the post-fauve movement. Sweeping in concept and size, the paintings of his last period revealed the use of evocative color and applications of angular shading that seemed to animate his floating images.

MEYER SCHAPIRO (1904-) b. Shavly, Lithuania
Art Critic Regarded by many as a singular voice in art criticism, he was said by *The New York Times* to have shaken the dust off art history and made the medieval as vivid as the modern. His lectures and writings were steeped in psychoanalytical and mystical references shedding light on the creative impulses behind great artists throughout time.

GEORGE SEGAL (1924-) b. New York City
Sculptor Admired for his audacity and vision, the abstract expressionist turned sculptor introduced a new American art form by casting white plaster figures from living human models. A leading member of the pop art movement, he often placed his haunting figures in settings of everyday life, such as subway and gas stations, kitchens and phone booths.

SAUL STEINBERG (1914-) b. Ramaicol-Sarat, Romania
Artist After a brief architectural career in Italy (1939-1941), he settled in New York and prospered as a watercolorist. But only as a cartoonist and political satirist for *The New Yorker* magazine did he gain national exposure and a large following. Seldom have the idiosyncracies of society been so sharply yet touchingly delineated than in his spare line drawings.

MAX WEBER (1881-1961) b. Bialystok, Russia
Artist His early work, largely extensions of fauvism and cubism, was maligned by critics and collectors as too modernistic. Greatly influenced by Cezanne, he gradually evolved a more accessible form of realism. He was best known for his colorful, expressionistic portraits of the dissolute and decadent inhabitants of New York City's social scene.

Other Noted Artists and Sculptors

Saul Baizerman	Max Beckman
Peter Blume	Mark DiSovera
Henry Dreyfuss	Jacob Epstein
Emil Fuchs	Milton Glaser
Enrico Glicenstein	Adolph Gottlieb
William Gropper	Samuel Halper
Minna Harkavy	Joseph Hirsch
Morris Kantor	Bernard Karfiol
Alex Katz	Moise Kisling
Franz Kline	Ben Koppman
Leon Kroll	Francis Kriss
Louis Loeb	Morris Louis
Peter Max	Jerome Meyers
Barnett Newman	Ernest Peixotto
Robert Rauchenberg	Moses Sawyer
Ben Shawn	Raphael Soyer
Maurice Sterne	Albert Sterner
Abraham Walkowitz	Nat Werner

Photographers and Photo Journalists

DIANE ARBUS (1923-71) b. New York City
Photographer The former fashion photographer abandoned the beautiful in the late 1950s for the grotesque world of drug addicts, prostitutes, circus freaks and the dead and dying. Her photography spoke to the dark side of consciousness and gained wide exposure through exhibits and publications. Her brother was the Pulitzer Prize-winning poet, Howard Nemerov.

RICHARD AVEDON (1923-) b. New York City
Photographer His innovative fusion of candid and studio photography raised commercial fashion photography to an art form. By the late 1960s his photographic journey found him recording world figures and celebrities as they were never seen before – in portraits of breathtaking honesty, most often immensely enlarged against white backgrounds.

CORNELL CAPA (1918-) b. Budapest, Hungary
Photographer The founder of the International Center of Photography (1974) turned to subject matter that made the craft of photography more relevant and reflective of contemporary life and art. He is the brother of photo journalist Robert Capa and an outstanding photographer in his own right, focusing largely on historical news and social events.

ROBERT CAPA (1910-1954) b. Budapest, Hungary
Photographer The world famous combat photographer brought home the agony and nightmare of war with sensitivity and compassion. A sharp eye for dramatic detail exalted his prize-winning coverage of the Spanish Civil War and World War Two. His death by a detonated mine during the Indo-China conflict was his ironic martyrdom to the subject he covered.

ALFRED STIEGLITZ (1864-1946) b. Hoboken, NJ
Photographer A master of his discipline, he was credited with establishing photography as an art form worthy of display in museums and galleries, and in general interest magazines. The innovative photographer edited *Camera Work* and was noted for his studies of New York City and many striking portraits of his wife, artist Georgia O'Keeffe.

Other Noted Photographers and Photo Journalists

Alfred Eisenstaedt
perfected the craft of photo journalism

Carl Mydans
photo journalist for the original *Life* magazine

Ruth Orkin
photographer of stars and celebrities

Joe Rosenthal
best known for his Iwo Jima flag-raising photo

Architects and Engineers

ALBERT KAHN (1869-1942) b. Rhaunen, Germany
Architect The builder of industrial structures employed reinforced concrete before it came into widespread use. He designed more than 1,000 buildings for Ford Motor Company and was retained by other automotive firms to construct assembly plants. He brought his expertise to Russia in 1930 and designed a network of factories to fulfill several of the nation's 5-year plans.

ELY KAHN (1884-1972) b. New York City

Architect The versatile and productive architect built housing complexes, office towers, public buildings, factories, department stores and hospitals. His designs were harmonious and clean, reflecting his dislike of disproportion and adornment. He was chairman of the Beaux Arts Institute of Design (1930) and authored *Design in Art and Industry* (1935).

LOUIS KAHN (1901-74) b. Osel, Estonia

Architect His international reputation for trend-setting design was partly based on his medical research building at the University of Pennsylvania (1960). Other noteworthy structures included the Kimball Art Museum and the Yale University art gallery. He also built housing projects and was a lively teacher with widespread influence on American architectural design.

Other Noted Architects and Engineers

Dankmar Adler
His steel frame buildings helped enable the age of sky-scrapers. Among his projects: Carnegie Hall in New York and the Chicago Stock Exchange.

Gordon Bunshaft
Designed New York City's Lever building, a forerunner of America's large scale office complexes.

Phyllis Lambert
Instrumental in retaining renowned architect Meis van der Rohe to design the landmark Seagram building in New York City.

David Steinman
Involved in the reconstruction of the Brooklyn Bridge and five-mile long Mackinac Bridge in Michigan.

Joseph Strauss
>   Designed the Golden Gate Bridge and 500 other bridges worldwide.

Also among eminent Jewish-American architectural designers and engineers of this century are:

Max Abramovitz	**Arnold Brunner**
Percival Goodman	**Charles Luckman**
Eric Mendleson	

Four
Stage, Screen and Television

Not until the Renaissance did Jews in central Europe begin to evolve a theatrical tradition entirely their own. At first, the stage filled with dramatic religious works performed in Yiddish and Hebrew. As the art gradually spread across the Continent, comedies were added to its repertoire, even as Jews occasionally appeared in gentile theater.

Like minstrels of earlier times, Jewish storytellers, vocalists, puppeteers and carnival clowns toured Jewish settlements and neighborhoods. Through the ages these entertainments inspired a theatrical culture which eventually influenced such performers as the late Sarah Bernhardt, Harry Houdini, Eddie Cantor, Bert Lahr, Fanny Brice and Al Jolson. A debt to that tradition is also owed by others like Jack Benny, George Burns, Ed Wynn, Danny Kaye and Milton Berle.

Modern Yiddish theater, a product of the late 19th Century, had roots in Romania and vibrant offshoots in New York City. Its radiance in America was soon to be dimmed by Jewish assimilation which favored English as the language of the stage. Paul Muni and Edward G. Robinson were among the most successful converts from the old world of floorboards and footlights to the new realm of the motion pictures.

The early evolution of the movie industry in America, run chiefly by Jewish entrepreneurs and artists, was a watershed for the Jew on stage. Silent films posed no language barriers, and the only essentials for stardom were the comedic pratfalls and emotional fireworks that caught the fancy of the public. These were the stock-in-trade of Yiddish actors who smoothly imported their theatrics into the new medium. Many like Charley Chaplin were inducted on the movie lot of the historic Universal Studios, founded in 1916 by Carl Laemmle.

The Jewish presence continued as motion pictures matured, and radio and television later became the nation's premier entertainment vehicles. What's more, the pioneering founders of the nation's three major radio and TV networks were also Jewish: David Sarnoff of NBC, William Paley of CBS and Leonard Goldenson of ABC.

The names of the many actors, directors, writers and executives of Jewish origin are legend.

Stage, Screen and TV Performers

TIM ALLEN (1953-) b. Denver, CO
Actor/Comedian In early career, the star of the top-rated, award-winning TV series *Home Improvement* was a stand-up comic, advertising agency executive and founder of a graphics design company. He was discovered on TV's *Showtime Comedy Club All-stars II (1988)*. His book *Don't Stand Too Close to a Naked Man* was published in 1994.

WOODY ALLEN (1935-) b. New York City
Actor/Writer/Director The nonconformist talent has won Oscars for *Annie Hall* (1977) and for *Hannah and Her Sisters* (1986). His leading characters often caricature neurotic urbanites struggling to cope with life's social and sexual predilections. He began as a gag writer for Sid Caesar's TV show in the 1950s, and continues to moonlight as a standup comic and jazz clarinetist.

BEATRICE ARTHUR (1924-) b. New York City
Actress/Singer As the forceful, opinionated lead in the hit TV series *Maude* (1972-78) she epitomized the liberated woman, earning an Emmy for that role. Earlier stage appearances as a comedienne and singer included parts in *The Threepenny Opera* and *Mame* for which she won a 1966 Tony Award. Her TV work in *Golden Girls* (1987-88) delivered a second Emmy.

LAUREN BACALL (1924-) b. New York City
Actress Her movie debut in *To Have and Have Not* (1944) announced a star whose aloof sensuality shined through other films including *The Big Sleep* (1946) and *Key Largo* (1948). She turned to comedy in *How to Marry a Millionaire* (1953), and to song in *Applause* (1970) for which she earned a Tony. Her four films with husband Humphrey Bogart cast them as screendom's torrid duo.

THEDA BARA (1890-1955) b. Cincinnati, OH
Actress She was the first femme fatale of silent cinema, an erotic star who introduced the word "vamp" into the vocabulary of sin. Her image on screen was described as that of "a depraved, merciless enslaver of men." "Kiss me, you fool!" from one of her forty films was an expression of the day as she became a forerunner of the heartless movieland seductress.

ROSEANNE BARR (1953-) b. Salt Lake City, UT
Comedienne/Actress Describing herself as a "domestic goddess," the star of her long-running sitcom *Roseanne* has attracted on and off screen attention satirizing marriage, children and housework. Since her show aired in 1988, it has become a controversial media subject and is regarded by some as New Wave, feminist or revolutionary, and always stimulating.

JACK BENNY (1894-1974) b. Waukegan, IL
Comedian Generations of Americans knew the self-effacing humor and antics of an endearing funny man whose radio and TV shows (1931-65) sparkled with his masterly comedic timing. A foremost comedian of his day, at times scraping away at a poorly played violin, he appeared in several dozen films including the Ernst Lubitsch classic *To Be or Not to Be* in 1942.

59

GERTRUDE BERG (1899-1966) b. New York City
Actress/Scriptwriter The ethnic radio serial she began writing and producing in 1929--*The Goldbergs*--ran weekly for nineteen years, soared in popularity and spawned many spinoffs. Acting in all her episodes as a wickedly wise and sentimental Jewish "mamaleh," she brought her character to Broadway in *Me and Molly* (1948) and then to TV for the medium's first record setter.

MILTON BERLE (1908-) b. New York City
Comedian Breaking away from vaudeville and radio, he became TV's precocious superstar gifted with non-stop energy and lightning-quick ad libs. "Mr. Television," alias "Uncle Miltie," dominated the TV ratings for years and remains in the public eye through guest appearances and occasional films. He was inducted into the International Comedy Hall of Fame in 1991.

MEL BLANC (1908-89) b. San Francisco, CA
Cartoon/Vocalist His elastic voice became that of myriad animated cartoon characters: Bugs Bunny, Daffy Duck, Porky Pig, Tweety Pie the canary, Woody Woodpecker, Elmer Fudd and a host of others. The "Man of 1000 Voices" appeared on the *Jack Benny Show*, often developed special sound effects, and established an advertising firm producing radio and TV commercials.

VICTOR BORGE (1909-) b. Copenhagen, Denmark
Comedian/Pianist This Danish transplant to the American stage abandoned a concert career to originate a comedic style of mirthful monologues accompanied by his piano antics. The much sought-after radio, TV and variety show guest also performs in his native country and has occasionally been featured in concert with leading symphony orchestras.

DAVID BRENNER (1945-) b. Philadelphia, PA
Comedian/Writer His anecdotal materials deal with the frustrations of everyday annoyances--striking a cross-cultural chord with a large following of TV talk show audiences and dinner club fans. He has also produced shows for TV stations in Chicago, Philadelphia and New York, and authored *Soft Pretzels with Mustard* and *Revenge is the Best Exercise* (1986).

FANNY BRICE 1891-1951) b. New York City
Singer/Comedienne A regular performer in the *Ziegfield Follies* and in vaudeville during the 1920s and 1930s, she later won millions of radio listeners as the inimitable Baby Snooks. The master of mimicry and dialect also appeared in six motion pictures. The 1964 musical comedy *Funny Girl*, based on her life, was adapted in 1968 for a film starring Barbra Streisand.

MEL BROOKS (1926-) b. New York City
Comedian/Screenwriter/Director His lusty brand of humor set new formulas for screen pranks and antics. The former writer for Sid Caesar's *Your Show of Shows* created the *Get Smart* TV series and won a screenplay Oscar for *The Producers* (1968). He also shares his broad and imaginative comedy on TV talk shows. Greatest hits: *Blazing Saddles* and *Young Frankenstein* (1974).

EDDIE CANTOR (1892-1964) b. New York City
Comedian/Singer One of the most engaging figures in entertainment brought his wide-eyed vitality to vaudeville in 1906 and became a Broadway regular in the *Ziegfeld Follies* from 1916 into the Forties. Sellout stage runs and coast-to-coast tours further endeared him to a large public. His appearances in films, on radio and in early TV were highly rated.

CHARLIE CHAPLIN (1889-1977) b. London, England
Actor The most indelible image on the silent screen was his tragi-comic tramp baffled by social convention in such gems as *The Gold Rush* (1925) and *City Lights* (1931). A uniquely gifted mime, writer and director, he helped found United Artists in 1919 and won a special Academy Award in 1973 for lifetime achievement. He was knighted by the English crown two years later.

LEE J. COBB (1911-76) b. New York City
Actor Those who saw him on Broadway in *The Death of a Salesman* (1949) will remember his wrenching performance as Willy Loman. Considered by many critics the best character actor of his time, he appeared in more than fifty films: *The Golden Boy* (1939), *Winged Victory* (1944), *Anna and the King of Siam* (1946), *On the Waterfront* (1954), *Twelve Angry Men* (1957) and *Exodus* (1960).

BILLY CRYSTAL (1947-) b. Long Beach, NY
Comedian/Actor/Director Regular slots on two TV comedy series, *Soap* (1977-81) and *Saturday Night Live* (1984-85), paved his way to stardom. The standup comic has collected Emmys for performing and writing, as well as laurels for roles in *When Harry Met Sally* (1989) and *City Slickers* (1991). He also hosted the Grammy Awards in 1989 and the Academy Award ceremony in 1991.

RODNEY DANGERFIELD (1922-) b. Babylon, NY
Comedian "I get no respect," is the refrain that mocks his long and successful career--first as a businessman, then as a nightclub owner and at all times the master of the snappy, self-mocking one-liners he made his own. He brought his frenetic routines to the screen and TV, and played in character in *Caddyshack* (1980) and in *Back to School* (1986).

SAMMY DAVIS, JR. (1925-90) b. New York City

Entertainer The convert to Judaism was "Mr. Wonderful" to millions of fans, a charismatic song-and-dance artist whose renditions of "Mr. Bojangles" and "Candy Man" were hits of their day. A crowd pleaser from age-three, he was a spirited stage, screen and TV performer, often for special causes. He worked courageously through illnesses to the end of his life.

KIRK DOUGLAS (1916-) b. Amsterdam, NY

Actor He achieved stardom as the remorseless fighter in *Champion* (1949) and became a box office favorite from then on. His impassioned depictions of driven men energized many classics among his nearly seventy films. Most memorable were *Lust for Life* (1956), *Paths of Glory* (1957) and *Sparticus* (1960). He recently published an autobiography and novel.

RICHARD DREYFUSS (1947-) b. New York City

Actor He alternates between stage and screen during a career whose film credits include leading roles in *American Graffiti* (1973), *Jaws* (1975) and an Oscar-winning performance in Neil Simon's *The Goodbye Girl* (1977). His intensity and theatricality also played to live audiences attending *Major Barbara* (1972), *Julius Caesar* (1978) and *Othello* (1979).

PETER FALK (1927-) b. New York City

Actor Since taking center stage in *Don Juan* (1956), the serio-comic performer has received a near-record four Emmys in episodes of his internationally syndicated TV series *Columbo* (1971-77). Not to be typecast as the rumpled police lieutenant who is deceptively muddled, the ex-Merchant Marine cook has also collected film credits for more than forty features.

MARTY FELDMAN (1933-82) b. London, England
Actor/Director He began his career as a touring comic before joining Mel Brooks and Gene Wilder, and co-starring in several of their films. He then branched out as a screen actor and director appearing in *Educating Archie*, and was best known as Igor in *Young Frankenstein* (1974) and as the film director of *The Last Remake of Beau Geste* (1977).

JACK GILFORD (1907-90) b. New York City
Actor/Comedian While more familiar to young filmgoers for appearances in the 1980's hits *Cocoon* and *Cocoon II*, older audiences will recall his cameos on the *Milton Berle Review* and in *A Funny Thing Happened on the Way to the Forum* (1966). He received several Tony nominations and Jack Lemmon's bravo as "one of the most talented" performers on stage and screen.

BUDDY HACKETT (1924-) b. New York City
Actor/Comedian This irrepressible wit who first worked the cafe and nightclub circuit gained national exposure on TV variety shows during the 1960s. An able impersonator with an agile face, he has also appeared in supporting roles in *God's Little Acre* (1958), *The Music Man* (1962), *It's a Mad, Mad, Mad, Mad World* (1963) and *The Love Bug* (1969).

GOLDIE HAWN (1945-) b. Washington, D.C.
Actress/Comedienne After graduating from winsome, slapstick roles on TV's *Laugh-in* (1968-70), she vaulted to stardom as a serio-comedic actress of substantial range. *Cactus Flower* (1969) earned her an Oscar as best supporting actress. She appeared in *Shampoo* (1975), *Private Benjamin* (1980), and in *Housesitter* and *Death Becomes Her* in the Nineties.

JUDD HIRSCH   (1935-)   b. New York City

Actor   He invested stage and TV roles with finesse and warmth that have twice earned Tony awards, as well as Obie, Emmy and Drama Desk prizes. He was the calm eye of the storm in the popular TV sitcom *Taxi* (1978-83) and in *Ordinary People* (1980). He later starred in the stage hits *I'm Not Rappaport* (1986) and *Conversations With My Father* (1992).

DUSTIN HOFFMAN   (1937-)   b. Los Angeles, CA

Actor   He had collected awards for stagecraft even before his convincing performances in *The Graduate* (1967) and in *Midnight Cowboy* (1969). Realizing his roles with depth and passion, he won Oscars for *Kramer vs. Kramer* (1979) and *Rain Man* (1988). His manic masquerade in the cross-dressing farce *Tootsie* earned a Golden Globe award in 1982.

JUDY HOLLIDAY   (1922-65)   b. New York City

Actress   Her performances as the blonde bubblehead in the stage and Oscar-winning screen versions of *Born Yesterday* (1946, 1950) belied her soaring 170-plus I.Q. in real life. Her appeal and wistful radiance before the cameras were repeated in ten films also including *Adam's Rib* (1949), *It Should Happen to You* (1954) and *The Solid Gold Cadillac* (1956).

HARRY HOUDINI   (1874-1926)   b. Budapest, Hungary

Entertainer   He escaped while handcuffed in locked safes under water, made elephants disappear on stage and threaded needles held in his mouth. The escape artist, magician and acrobat earned an unchallenged reputation, and went on to expose mediums and fortune tellers who prey on the public. His personal library on magic is a prized collection in the Library in Congress.

GEORGE JESSEL (1898-1981) b. New York City
Comedian/Producer During an eventful 70-year career, he captured Broadway as a performer and producer of hit musicals, a feat he repeated in Hollywood in the 1940s and 1950s. He gained equal fame presiding at fund raising dinners which netted huge donations for worthy causes, and was accordingly awarded the title "Toastmaster General of the United States."

AL JOLSON (1886-1950) b. Seredzius, Lithuania
Singer/Comedian He was showbiz itself, dominating vaudeville and musical theater for three decades. A star of film and radio as well, the magnetic performer with a resounding voice brought down the house with "Swanee" and "My Mammy," his signature songs. Movieland came of age with its first talkie *The Jazz Singer* (1927) in which he enacted a life story similar to his own.

MADELINE KAHN (1942-) b. Boston, MA
Actress/Singer The often raunchy comedienne and pop vocalist excels in scene-stealing film roles, typified by *Blazing Saddles* and *Young Frankenstein*, both released in 1974 by Mel Brooks. The zany satirist with operatic training who also performed in musical comedy, is a regular on talk TV and won a best actress Tony award in the play *The Sisters Rosenzweig* (1993).

DANNY KAYE (1913-87) b. New York City
Actor/Singer A spellbinding comedian, he captivated audiences with his rapid-fire delivery of songs, satire and mimicry mellowed by humility. The most unforgettable of his fifteen films include *The Secret Life of Walter Mitty* (1947) and *Hans Christian Anderson* (1952). He was also a globe-trotting emissary for the United Nations International Children's Emergency Fund.

ALAN KING (1927-) b. New York City
Comedian/Actor/Producer He graduated from the Catskill "borscht belt" and night club gigs in the 1940s to successes on Broadway, in Hollywood and on TV. The author of three books also co-starred with Ali McGraw in *Tell Me What You Want* (1980) and produced several films. He formerly chaired the NY State Film Commission and is part owner of the Kaufman-Astoria Studios, NY.

JACK KLUGMAN (1922-) b. Philadelphia, PA
Actor He honed his acting skills in such plays as *Saint Joan*, *Mister Roberts* and in the original Broadway production of *Gypsy*. But his greatest triumph was as the unkempt and likeable Oscar Madison opposite Tony Randall in *The Odd Couple*, the 1970-75 TV hit series which delivered two of his three Emmys. He also played the crusty coroner in TV's *Quincy, M.E.* (1976-83).

MARTIN LANDAU (1931-) b. New York City
Actor The versatile performer, often cast in sinister roles, capped his appearances in 25 films with a 1995 Oscar for his supporting role in *Ed Wood*. Equally active on TV, he was a dramatic presence on *Mission Impossible* (1966-69) and *Space: 1999* (1975-77). The seasoned actor came to Hollywood from *The New York Daily News* for which he once worked as a staff cartoonist.

OSCAR LEVANT (1906-72) b. Pittsburgh, PA
Entertainer/Pianist/Composer He was prominently linked with George Gershwin, a close friend whose piano compositions he concertized on stage and in film. Moviegoers who knew his sharp repartee might recall the songs he composed for *Street Girl* (1929) and *Music is Magic* (1935). He also wrote jazz and orchestral pieces, and several withering autobiographies.

67

JERRY LEWIS (1926-) b. Newark, NJ

Actor/Producer/Writer The irrepressible comedian's night club antics with Dean Martin in the 1940s were recreated in sixteen of their films. After their 1956 parting, he wrote and directed for stage and cinema. He played leads in *The King of Comedy* (1983), and in TV's *Wiseguys* (1990), and has been the Muscular Dystrophy Foundation's spokesperson since 1950.

SHARI LEWIS (1934-) b. New York City

Puppeteer Children of all ages were charmed for three decades by her joshing dialogues with her TV creations, Lamb Chop, Hush Puppy and Charley Horse. Their appearances in the early 1960s on the *Shari Lewis Show* were reborn in 1992 on PBS TV. She has also produced children's books, videotapes and recordings, and has made guest appearances on TV variety and game shows.

HAL LINDEN (1931-) b. New York City

Actor/Singer The versatile entertainer—first as a vocalist with big bands—turned to acting in Broadway's *The Bells are Ringing* (1958). He won a Tony for the musical *The Rothschilds* in 1971 and later starred in the acclaimed TV series *Barney Miller* (1975-82). He has since appeared in the serial *Jack's Place* and on TV guest shows and specials.

PETER LORRE (1904-64) b. Rozsahegy, Hungary

Actor With his characteristic air of repressed menace, he starred in Fritz Lang's European film chiller *M* before coming to the U.S. and appearing in Alfred Hitchcock's *The Man Who Knew Too Much* (1934). He played the Japanese detective, Mr. Moto, in eight films during the late 1930s, and was best known for parts in *The Maltese Falcon* (1941) and *Casablanca* (1942).

MARX BROTHERS   Film career: 1929-59
Comedy Team Vaudeville and the films never saw their like: the zaniness and chaos wreaked by the caustic, wisecracking Groucho, the pantomime of the mute harpist, Harpo, the language-mangling pianist, Chico, and the straight man and vocalist, Zeppo. Their all-time movie hits include *Animal Crackers* (1930), *Duck Soup* (1933), *A Night at the Opera* (1935) and *Room Service* (1938).

GROUCHO MARX   (1890-1977) b. New York City
Entertainer Following the breakup of the Marx Brothers team, he went his own way in the 1940s, hosting with his usual zeal the radio and TV versions of *You Bet Your Life*--a pioneering quiz show of its kind. He also appeared in several films and frequented the channels as a roisterous guest. The off-stage intellect of gentleness and charm authored many whimsical books.

WALTER MATTHAU   (1920-) b. New York City
Actor At home on stage, screen and TV, mostly in comic roles, the often gruff and disheveled actor earned an early Oscar for *The Fortune Cookie* (1966), and credits for more than fifty film appearances. At peak career, he starred in adaptations of Neil Simon's Broadway hits--in *The Odd Couple* (1968), *Plaza Suite* (1971) and *The Sunshine Boys* (1975).

ELAINE MAY   (1932-) b. Philadelphia, PA
Actress/Screenwriter/Director Long paired with Mike Nichols in improvisational comedy, she went on to success in multiple fields: as an actress in *Enter Laughing* (1966) and *Luv* (1967), as a writer of *Such Good Friends* (1971) and as the director of *The Heartbreak Kid* (1972). She and Nichols also co-starred in a restaging of *Who's Afraid of Virginia Wolf* in 1980.

BETTE MIDLER (1945-) b. Honolulu, Hawaii
Actress/Comedienne/Singer Her debut in *Fiddler on the Roof* later landed nightclub billings for the stylist whose bawdy songs and comic routines gained a large following. A regular on TV, she won a 1972 Grammy for a first album and an Oscar nomination for *The Rose* (1979). Other credits include *Outrageous Fortune* (1987) and *Scenes from a Mall* with Woody Allen (1991).

MARILYN MONROE (1926-62) b. Los Angeles, CA
Actress/Comedienne The sex goddess projected sensuous innocence in her nearly thirty films, as well as in her off-screen life. Associated with the rich and famous, she was nevertheless an earnest performer with comedic and dramatic talent in *Gentlemen Prefer Blondes* (1953), *Bus Stop* (1957) and *The Misfits* (1961). She converted to Judaism on marriage to playwright Arthur Miller.

HENRY MORGAN (1915-94) b. New York City
Radio/TV Personality Scathing wit and spoofs were trademarks of the legendary bad boy of New York radio whose first show *Here's Morgan* debuted in the early 1940s. He mocked sponsors and ad libbed a style of satirical humor well ahead of its time. In 1963, the master of mimicry became a regular panelist on TV's *I've Got a Secret* for fourteen years.

ZERO MOSTEL (1915-77) b. New York City
Actor/Comedian A role in *DuBarry Was a Lady* (1943) introduced the commanding actor with an imposing physique and instinct for comedic delivery. His greatest hits were on Broadway in *A Funny Thing Happened on the Way to the Forum* (1963) and *Fiddler on the Roof* (1964). Accolades also came for his performance in the Mel Brooks film *The Producers* (1967).

PAUL MUNI (1895-1967) b. Lemberg, Austria
Actor The veteran of Yiddish theater made a natural conversion to the American stage and screen with portrayals in *The Story of Louis Pasteur* (1936) that earned an Oscar, and in *Inherit the Wind* (1955) that won a Tony. Others among his 23 films were *Scarface* (1932), *I Am a Fugitive from a Chain Gang* (1932), *The Life of Emile Zola* (1937) and *The Last Angry Man* (1959).

LUISE RAINER (1910-95) b. Vienna, Austria
Actress Successive Oscars for touching performances in *The Great Ziegfeld* (1936) and *The Good Earth* (1937) capped her brief motion picture career which ended with *Hostages* in 1943. Upon retirement she occasionally appeared on stage and TV, and applied time and considerable artistic talent to painting. She was once married to playwright Clifford Odets.

TONY RANDALL (1920-) b. Tulsa, OK
Actor/Director Emmy-winning actor, director, TV celebrity, impresario and art collector, he is best known as the fastidious Felix of *The Odd Couple* in its long-run TV and theatrical productions. He has appeared in more than thirty films, is a TV regular on the *Texaco Opera Quiz* and has launched The National Actors Theatre which stages the world's greatest plays.

CARL REINER (1923-) b. New York City
Actor/Comedian/Screenwriter His 1947 Broadway opening in *Call Me Mister* began a show business career with few parallels. The gifted humorist and writer won most of his nine Emmys for Sid Caesar's *Your Show of Shows* in the 1950s and *The Dick Van Dyke Show* in the 1960s. He also collected directing credits for four Steve Martin features and other films.

ROB REINER   (1945-)   b. New York City
Actor/Director/Producer/Screenwriter   The son of Carl Reiner won two Emmys while a mainstay with the long-running TV series *All in the Family* before turning to motion picture production and direction. He has occasionally appeared in cameo screen roles and directed several critical successes including *The Princess Bride* (1986) and *When Harry Met Sally* (1989).

RITZ BROTHERS   Film Career: 1936-75
Comedy Team   For decades, Al, Jimmy and Harry strutted their wild buffoonery in vaudeville and pictures, influencing future purveyors of slapstick and mime like Danny Kaye, Jerry Lewis and Sid Caesar. The trio began filming with Alice Faye in *Sing, Baby, Sing* (1936) and retired from the screen with Harry's solo appearance in Mel Brooks' 1975 comedy hit *Silent Movie*.

JOAN RIVERS   (1933-)   b. New York City
Comedienne/Author   Her outrageous ad libs and self-mockery earned frequent guest spots on Johnny Carson's *Tonight Show* which she sometimes hosted (1983-86). Soon after, she conducted her own late-night show, then debuted a successful morning talk show in 1989. Her writings include *The Life and Hard Times of Heidi Abromowitz* (1984) and *Enter Talking* (1986).

EDWARD G. ROBINSON   (1893-1973)   b. Bucharest, Rumania
Actor   His early type casting as a gangster--typically in *Little Caesar* (1931)--mellowed in later films including *Dr. Ehrlich's Magic Bullet* (1940), *All My Sons* (1948), *The Prize* (1964) and *Soylent Green* (1973). He starred in more than ninety films and thirty stage productions. In private life, the often imitated actor was a talented painter, art collector and linguist.

72

MORT SAHL (1927-) b. Montreal, Canada
Satirist/Writer Derisive monologues during nightclub, stage and college tours over the decades gained a loyal audience for the sharp-tongued iconoclast with a hectic delivery. He targeted the hypocrisies of politicians and foibles of pop culture, and shared his wit on his own TV show *The Mort Sahl Special* (1960). He has also appeared in films and has written satirical magazine articles.

JERRY SEINFELD (1954-) b. New York City
Actor/Comedian His top-rated TV series *Seinfeld* gathers a close-knit group of young adult friends grappling with the frustrations of life and love, and has been called a "cultural signpost for relationships in the 1990s." His rapid banter, whetted by years of stand-up comedy, makes him a prized talk show guest. His most recent bestseller was *Seinlanguage* (1993).

PHIL SILVERS (1912-85) b. New York City
Actor/Comedian His depiction of Sergeant Bilko, the exuberant and approachable lead in *The Phil Silvers Show* (1955-58), moved the three-time Emmy-winning TV series to the top of the charts. He also appeared in more than thirty films during a forty year career, and won stage credits for roles in *High Button Shoes* (1947) and a Tony award for *Top Banana* (1951).

BARBRA STREISAND (1942-) b. New York City
Actress/Singer/Director *Funny Girl* (1942) was a stepping stone to superstardom for the entertainer who won an Oscar in its film version. Emmy and Grammy awards came with TV specials, concerts and recordings by the actress who has recently directed and produced feature films. She starred in *Hello Dolly!* (1969), *The Way We Were* (1973), *A Star is Born* (1976) and *Yentl* (1983).

ELIZABETH TAYLOR (1932-) b. London, England

Actress During a high profile career, the endearing child actress in *National Velvet* (1944) came into her own as a glamorous, dazzling international celebrity. The convert to Judaism was nominated for three Academy Awards before winning Oscars for her role in *Butterfield 8* (1960) and for a blistering performance in *Who's Afraid of Virginia Woolf* (1966).

THE THREE STOOGES Film Career: 1934-58

Comedy Team More than 200 short films erupted with the wild, brawling slapstick humor of the masters of comedic invention: brothers Moe, Shemp and Curly Howard with a one-time stand-in, Larry Fine. Despite minor cast changes, they remained a cohesive group bringing the hijinx and antics of vaudeville to the screen, inspiring successors like Abbott and Costello.

ELI WALLACH (1915-) b. New York City

Actor Since his first Broadway break in 1945, few stage or screen seasons were without performances by the versatile artist. His career took off with an appearance in *Mister Roberts* (1949), a Tony for *The Rose Tattoo* (1951) and an Emmy for *The Poppy is Also a Flower* (1966). Often teamed with his actress wife, Anne Jackson, he has brought his robust style to over 100 productions.

GENE WILDER (1935-) b. Milwaukee, WI

Actor/Screenwriter *Bonnie and Clyde* (1967) was the first and only dramatic vehicle for the graduate of the Actors Studio and Old Vic Theatre. He adopted comedy, joined Mel Brooks and debuted in *The Producers* (1967). He also co-wrote and appeared in *Young Frankenstein* and *Blazing Saddles* (1974). Parodies of romances, comedies, westerns and detective films are his media.

HENRY WINKLER (1945-) b. New York City
Actor/Producer He will forever be "Fonzi" for his quasi tough-guy role in the long-running TV series *Happy Days* (1974-85). His screen appearance in *The Lords of Flatbush* (1974) was equally memorable. He was also the executive producer of TV's popular adventure series *MacGyver* (1985-92) and is a dedicated campaigner for humanitarian causes on behalf of children.

SHELLEY WINTERS (1923-) b. St. Louis, MO
Actress More than forty years before the cameras have earned her Oscars for best supporting actress in *The Diary of Anne Frank* (1959) and in *A Patch of Blue* (1965). She is also a spiky TV talk show guest with stage credits as well, and has won praise for screen roles in *A Place in the Sun* (1951), *Executive Suite* (1954), *Lolita* (1962) and *The Poseidon Adventure* (1972).

ED WYNN (1886-1966) b. Philadelphia, PA
Actor/Comedian The personable and often clownish media star drew raves since his 1932 entry on radio as *The Fire Chief*, succeeded by the TV variety series *The Ed Wynn Show*. He won TV's first Emmy for an Outstanding Live Personality, and was the first to spoof sponsors' commercials. His several dramatic roles in films included a part in *The Diary of Anne Frank* (1959).

Other Noted Stage, Screen and TV Performers

Alan Arkin	**Edward Arnold**
Edward Asner	**Martin Balsam**
Richard Benjamin	**Theodore Bikel**
Joan Blondell	**Tom Bosley**
Edward Bromberg	**Geraldine Brooks**

James Caan	Dyan Cannon
Kitty Carlisle	Jeff Chandler
Jill Clayburgh	Robert Clary
Tony Curtis	Melvyn Douglas
Arlene Francis	Martin Gabel
John Garfield	Hermione Gingold
Paulette Goddard	Gary David Goldberg
Elliot Gould	Virginia Graham
Lee Grant	Lorne Greene
Joel Grey	Anna Held
Sam Jaffe	Francine Larrimore
Louise Lasser	Sheldon Leonard
Lotte Lenya	Sam Levene
Tina Louise	Paul Lukas
Janet Margolin	Phyllis Newman
Leonard Nimoy	Lilli Palmer
Molly Picon	Winona Ryder
Molly Ringwald	Lillian Roth
Rudolf Schildkraut	Maurice Schwartz
George Segal	William Shatner
Norma Shearer	Sylvia Sidney
Jill St. John	Rod Steiger
Sam Wanamaker	Debra Winger
Efrem Zimbalist, Jr.	

Other Noted Comics and Humorists

Don Adams	Joey Adams
Marty Allen	Morey Amsterdam

Phil Baker	Shelley Berman
Joey Bishop	Lenny Bruce
Red Buttons	Jack Carter
Myron Cohen	"Professor" Irwin Corey
Norman Crosby	Bill Dana
Totie Fields	Phil Foster
Mickey Freeman	Stan Friedberg
David Frye	Jackie Gayle
Jack Gilford	Shecky Greene
Gabe Kaplan	Marvin Kaplan
Mickey Katz	Stubby Kaye
Robert Klein	Bert Lahr
Pinky Lee	Jack E. Leonard
Sheldon Leonard	Sam Levene
Sam Levenson	Jackie Mason
Anne Meara	Richard Meltzer
Marilyn Michaels	Howard Morris
Jan Murray	Louie Nye
Rhea Perlman	Don Rickles
Freddie Roman	Soupy Sales
Garry Shandling	Dick Shawn
Allan Sherman	Smith and Dale
Arnold Stang	David Steinberg
Jerry Stiller	Larry Storch
Wayne and Shuster	Weber and Fields
Henny Youngman	

Playwrights and Screenwriters

BERTOLT BRECHT (1898-1956) b. Augsburg, Germany
Playwright The Threepenny Opera (1928) with music by Kurt Weill was the best known work of a playwright and poet whose themes frequently dealt with poverty and suffering. His forty year career produced offerings with social content including *Jungle of Cities* (1923), *A Man's a Man* (1926), *St. Joan of the Stockyards* (1932) and *Mother Courage and Her Children* (1941).

ABE BURROWS (1910-85) b. New York City
Playwright/Director/Humorist The sly wit with a gravelly voice was a showman of all trades. He scripted radio and TV's *Duffy's Tavern* (1941-45) and the Broadway plays *Guys and Dolls* (1951) and *How to Succeed in Business Without Really Trying* (1961) for which he won a Pulitzer Prize. He also performed his spoofs and songs on his own radio show and during TV guest appearances.

PADDY CHAYEFSKY (1923-81) b. New York City
Playwright/Screenwriter Eloquent and sometimes scathing plays including *The Tenth Man, Gideon* and *The Latent Heterosexual* established his dramatic credentials. *Marty*, adapted from his TV script, earned a 1955 best film Academy Award. *The Bachelor Party* (1957), also an early hit, was followed by biting works that won Oscars: *The Hospital* (1971) and *Network* (1976).

BETTY COMDEN (1916-1994) b. New York City
Playwright/Screenwriter She formed the cabaret act *The Reviewers* with Judy Holliday and Adolph Green in 1939, and later co-wrote the book and lyrics for Broadway's *On the Town* (1944). She won five Tonys and numerous other awards with Green, her lifetime partner. Together they scripted *Singing in the Rain* (1952), considered by many as the greatest musical ever filmed.

NORA EPHRON (1941-) b. New York City
Screenwriter/Novelist/Director A novelist and screenwriter of equally high rank, she wrote *Heartburn* (1983) and a film script with Alice Arden for *Silkwood* (1983). She also co-produced *When Harry Met Sally* (1989) and scripted *Sleepless in Seattle* (1993). Her works often probed the motivations of independent women rebelling against authority.

JULES FEIFFER (1929-) b. New York City
Playwright/Cartoonist He and his dual talents received several acknowledgements: praise as the "most promising playwright of the 1966-67 season" from the NY Drama Critics, and a Pulitzer Prize for political cartooning in 1986. His satirical cartoons often depict neurotics wrestling with rejection. He staged *Little Murders* (1967) and *Carnal Knowledge* (1970).

MOSS HART (1904-61) b. New York City
Playwright His name and that of collaborator George S. Kaufman were synonymous with Broadway comedy for S.R.O. hits including *Once in a Lifetime* (1930), *Merrily We Roll Along* (1934) and *The Man Who Came to Dinner* (1939). He won Pulitzer Prizes for *You Can't Take it With You* (1936) and the musical *Lady in the Dark* which was written in 1941 with Kurt Weill and Ira Gershwin.

BEN HECHT (1893-1964) b. New York City
Playwright/Director A master of his craft, he won a 1927 Oscar for *Underworld*, and another for *The Scoundrel* in 1935. He produced sophisticated comedies, romances and mysteries through the 1930s and 1940s. Among other screenplays he wrote or adapted were *Nothing Sacred* (1937), Emily Bronte's *Wuthering Heights* (1939) and Alfred Hitchcock's *Notorious* (1946).

79

LILLIAN HELLMAN (1905-84) b. New Orleans, LA
Playwright/Screenwriter Her gripping plays of the 1930s and 1940s struck a note for moral responsibility in public and private life. *The Children's Hour* (1934), *The Little Foxes* (1939) and *Watch on the Rhine* (1941) were among the most popular and enduring of the more than a dozen dramas she wrote--a number of which she later adapted for motion pictures.

GARSON KANIN (1912-) b. Rochester, NY
Screenwriter/Playwright/Director The assistant stage director for the legendary George Abbott entered film making when brought to Hollywood by Samuel Goldwyn. He often collaborated with his wife, actress-writer Ruth Gordon, and directed her in *Adam's Rib* (1949). His strong, brawny screenplays for George Cukor and others placed him in the Theater Hall of Fame in 1985.

GEORGE S. KAUFMAN (1889-1961) b. Pittsburgh, PA
Playwright His name was on theater marquees for 35 years during which he earned Pulitzer Prizes for *Of Thee I Sing* (1932) and *You Can't Take it With You* (1936). In partnership with Moss Hart, Edna Ferber and others, he achieved more than thirty stage successes, many scripted for the films. Among them were *Stage Door* (1936) and *The Late George Apley* (1944).

HOWARD KOCH (1902-95) b. New York City
Screenwriter/Playwright His early adaptation *The War of the Worlds* (1938) was a realistic Orson Wells Mercury Theater radio drama that incited coast-to-coast panic. After arriving in Hollywood, he wrote screenplays for Warner Brothers, including *The Letter* (1940) and *Letter From an Unknown Woman* (1948). He also co-scripted the film masterpiece *Casablanca* in 1942.

80

DAVID MAMET (1947-) b. Chicago, IL
Playwright/Screenwriter A 1984 Pulitzer Prize was among three prestigious awards won by his cynical and savage play *Glengarry Glen Ross* (1984) which he later adapted for the screen. His first, equally notable Broadway play *American Buffalo* was produced in 1976. Other screenwriting credits include *The Postman Always Rings Twice* (1979) and *The Untouchables* (1987).

ARTHUR MILLER (1915-) b. New York City
Playwright He lit up Broadway with the Critic's Circle Award-winning *All My Sons* (1947). Further acclaim and a Pulitzer Prize were accorded to his American classic *The Death of a Salesman* (1949). Other plays and films include *The Crucible* (1953), *A View from the Bridge* (1955), *The Misfits* (1961) and *After the Fall* (1963), inspired by ex-wife, Marilyn Monroe.

CLIFFORD ODETS (1906-63) b. Philadelphia, PA
Playwright/Director Set in the Great Depression, his early plays exposed the plight of poverty's victims. Among his best known are the frequently revived *Waiting for Lefty* (1935) and *Golden Boy* (1931). Turning to films, he wrote screenplays for *The General Died at Dawn* (1936), *The Big Knife* (1955) and *None But the Lonely Heart* (1944) which he also directed.

ELMER RICE (1892-1967) b. New York City
Playwright A major figure in the world of theater for nearly a generation, he wrote expressionistic dramas, vividly drawn in his signature play *The Adding Machine* (1923). Others included the vintage *Street Scene* (1921) and *Counselor at Law* (1931). The lawyer turned writer was also active in the civil rights movement to which he contributed legal expertise.

NEIL SIMON (1927-) b. New York City
Playwright/Screenwriter No other contemporary playwright has scored more Broadway triumphs and successful TV and film adaptations. He often favors urban settings for his outpouring of wit and wisdom. *Barefoot in the Park* (1967), *The Odd Couple* (1968), *Biloxi Blues* (1988 Tony Award) and *Lost in Yonkers* (1991 Pulitzer Prize) are examples.

WENDY WASSERSTEIN (1950-) b. New York City
Playwright/Screenwriter Her work has been praised as droll and incisive, springing from issues of gender alienation. She carried that theme into one of Broadway's longest-running plays, *The Heidi Chronicles* (1989), winner of a Pulitzer Prize and Tony award. The 1992 opening of the witty *The Sisters Rosensweig* confirmed her as a playwright of formidable talent.

Other Noted Playwrights and Screenwriters

Leopold Atlas	Robert Bloch
Marshall Brickman	I.A.L. "Izzy" Diamond
Henry Ephron	Philip Epstein
Rose Franken	Sidney Kingsley
Arthur Laurents	Herman Mankewicz
Bella and Samuel Spewack	Rita Weiman
John Wexley	Susan Yankowitz

Directors, Producers, Executives and Impresarios

STELLA ADLER (1902-92) b. New York City
Director/Acting Teacher She was born into a famous theatrical family including her father Jacob and brother Luther. As a teacher, she modified the "Strasberg Method" in training dawning stars including Marlon Brando, Warren Beatty and Robert De Niro. She also founded a conservatory in which she taught, directed and acted, and she instructed at Yale and New York Universities.

ROBERT ALTMAN (1925-) b. Kansas City, MO
Director Following his first critical success *M*A*S*H* (1970) the film maker displayed remarkable virtuosity, extending from the comic to the dramatic to the irreverent. He has since produced the panoramic *Nashville* in 1975, *Streamers*, a saga of the Vietnam War (1983), *Vincent and Theo*, a 1990 chronicle of the Van Goghs, and his 1992 satire of Hollywood, *The Player*.

BARNEY BALABAN (1887-1971) b. Chicago, IL
Motion Picture Executive While in his early twenties, he introduced sloped floors, plush seats, balconies and air cooling in movie theaters. Paramount Pictures bought two-thirds of his majestic new theaters and elected him to its presidency in 1936. He also promoted wide screen projection and piloted his company into the emerging TV industry.

DAVID BELASCO (1859-1931) b. San Francisco, CA
Producer/Playwright Spectacular stage effects using lighting, animals and props were originated by the foremost dramatist of his time. Several theaters bearing his name showcased more than 370 of his lavish productions into the 1930s. He also wrote and staged *Madame Butterfly* (1900) and *The Girls of the Golden West* (1905), both transformed into operas by Giacomo Puccini.

PANDRO S. BERMAN (1905-) b. Pittsburgh, PA
Producer   He learned his vocation as an assistant director at Universal, and afterward produced some of Hollywood's landmark films for RKO and MGM: *The Hunchback of Notre Dame* (1939), *Sweet Bird of Youth* (1961), *Top Hat* (1935) and *The Blackboard Jungle* (1955). His homage from colleagues included the David O. Selznick Lifetime Achievement Award for Motion Pictures.

HARRY COHN (1891-1958) b. New York City
Motion Picture Executive   Entering the studio turmoil of Hollywood's early days, he joined brother Jack and Joe Brandt in a resolute drive to form Columbia Pictures (1924). He then pressed for and achieved a takeover of the company and guided it to success and profitability by retaining many promising stars, screenwriters and directors.

MARVIN DAVIS (1925-) b. Newark, NJ
Motion Picture Executive   He amassed a fortune in the oil business during the 1940s and applied it to a lifelong ambition— developing major entities in the entertainment industry. He first formed Neufield-Davis Productions and soon after acquired 20th Century-Fox (1981). Within three years he became the sole owner of Fox, half of which was later sold to Rupert Murdock.

BARRY DILLER (1942-) b. San Francisco, CA
Producer/Media Executive   His programming creativity helped gain prime-time command for ABC-TV during the 1960s and 1970s. He also brainstormed the mini-series concept and acquired rights to the record-shattering *Roots* (1977). Later, as CEO of Paramount (1974-84), he produced *Star Trek—the Motion Picture* (1979), *Urban Cowboy* (1980) and *Terms of Endearment* (1983).

MICHAEL EISNER (1942-) b. Mt. Kisco, NY
Motion Picture Executive The president of the worldwide Disney kingdom joined the company in 1985 after holding top posts at ABC-TV and Paramount Pictures. Adding his broad media experience to a collaboration with Jeffrey Katzenberg and Frank Wells (then CEO at Disney), he steered the company into an era of affluence with revenues from videos, theme parks and resort complexes.

MILOS FORMAN (1932-) b. Caslav, Czechoslovakia
Director The foreign-born film maker participated in his homeland's New Wave movement of the 1960s and produced the international hits, *The Loves of a Blonde* (1966) and *The Fireman's Ball* (1967). When in America, he won Oscars for *One Flew Over the Cuckoo's Nest* (1975) and *Amadeus* (1984). *Hair* in 1979 and *Ragtime* in 1981 were also among his notable pictures.

WILLIAM FOX (1879-1952) b. Tulchva, Hungary
Motion Picture Executive Nine years after founding a prosperous penny arcade business, he set his sights on Hollywood and formed the Fox Film Corporation--integrating production, exhibition and distribution. The company flourished in the 1920s with such hits as the Oscar-winning *Cavalcade* (1932), but folded four years after to reemerge as 20th Century Fox.

SIDNEY FRANKLIN (1893-1972) b. San Francisco, CA
Director/Producer He produced the Oscar-winning *Mrs. Miniver* (1942), *The Guardsman*--starring the legendary theater couple, Lunt and Fontanne--and *The Yearling* (1946). He was considered a scrupulous technician with refinement, skills he applied to other film classics including *Private Lives* (1931) and the original and remake of *The Barretts of Wimpole Street* (1934 and 1956).

DAVID GEFFEN (1943-) b. New York City
Producer/Agent An uncanny ability to discover and promote musical talent buttressed his successes in the recording industry and with film and theatrical properties. His long-running *Cats* (1983) and *M Butterfly* (1988) won Tony Awards. He is currently a member of the trio, including Steven Spielberg and Jeffrey Katzenberg, heading Dreamworks SKG Studio.

SAMUEL GOLDWYN (1882-1974) b. Warsaw, Poland
Producer The unchallenged giant of the film industry brought audiences such stars as Ronald Coleman, Gary Cooper, Will Rogers, David Niven and Merle Oberon. His generations of masterly and often opulent features included *The Squaw Man* (1913), *Wuthering Heights* (1939), *The Little Foxes* (1941), *The Best Years of Our Lives* (1947), *Guys and Dolls* (1955) and *Porgy and Bess* (1959).

RICHARD HEFFNER (1925-) b. New York City
Motion Picture Executive He served as chairman of the Classification and Rating Administration (1974-94), the voluntary motion picture rating system which helps parents guide their children's choice of films. He was also the first manager of Channel 13, the educational TV station he helped acquire, and currently hosts the respected TV series *The Open Mind*.

SOL HUROK (1890-1974) b. Pogar, Russia
Impresario America's most enterprising promoter and manager of performing artists and cultural events brought a wealth of talent to the international stage: Isadora Duncan, Benny Goodman, Maria Callas, the Bolshoi Ballet and many others. He was also instrumental in negotiating cultural exchange programs of mutual benefit between the U.S. and U.S.S.R.

JEFFREY KATZENBERG (1950-) b. New York City
Motion Picture Executive His spectacular rise within Paramount's movie and television operations climaxed in the chairmanship of Disney Studios at age 34. With Michael Eisner and Frank Wells, "the boy wonder" helped expand Disney's horizons with films appealing to older audiences. He left in 1994 to form Dreamworks SKG Studio with Steven Spielberg and David Geffen.

LINCOLN KIRSTEIN (1907-) b. Rochester, NY
Impresario/Writer He is a propagator of contemporary dance who founded the American Ballet with George Balanchine in 1934. Two years later he established Ballet Caravan to debut American works including Aaron Copland's *Billy the Kid* (1938) for which he wrote the libretto. He also helped form the Ballet Society, later renamed the New York City Ballet.

STANLEY KRAMER (1913-) b. New York City
Director/Producer/Screenwriter Moral and social concerns were addressed in many of his intelligent, compelling films. *Judgement at Nuremberg* (1961) dissected genocide, and *The Defiant Ones* (1958) and *Guess Who's Coming to Dinner* (1967) examined racial conflicts. Other films include *High Noon* (1953), *The Caine Mutiny* (1954), *On the Beach* (1959) and *Inherit the Wind* (1960).

ARTHUR KRIM (1910-) b. New York City
Motion Picture Executive The practicing lawyer became president of United Artists in 1951 and rejuvenated the studio which then issued motion picture standards such as *High Noon* (1952), *Marty* (1953) and *West Side Story* (1961). After time spent in national politics during the JFK era, he formed Orion Pictures (1978) and produced Oscar winners including *Annie Hall* (1977) and *Amadeus* (1984).

STANLEY KUBRICK (1928-) b. New York City
Director/Producer Working in England since 1961, the American-born movie director of daring originality produced *Paths of Glory*, a 1957 tour de force. Other prominent pictures include *Lolita* (1962), *Dr. Strangelove* (1964), *2001: A Space Odyssey* (1968) and *A Clockwork Orange* (1971). His films tend to treat moral and social issues with honesty and courage.

CARL LAEMMLE (1867-1939) b. Laupheim, Germany
Motion Picture Executive/Producer The founder of Universal Studios guided his company to several industry firsts: the full-length feature film, *Traffic in Souls* (1913), and the "star system" which lionized actors. Before forming a production company—the forerunner to Universal--he had acquired and operated a network of theaters in Chicago.

JESSE LASKY (1880-1958) b. San Francisco, CA
Motion Picture Executive He was among the first to appreciate the value of mergers in developing and expanding the industry. Jesse Lasky Features Play Company was formed in 1913 with brother-in-law Samuel Goldwyn and Cecille B. DeMille. It produced the epochal *Squaw Man* (1914), then merged with Adolph Zukor's film company, leading to the formation of Paramount.

NORMAN LEAR (1922-) b. New Haven, CT
Producer/Director/Writer The creator of the modern sitcom emerged in the 1950s as a comedy hour writer, then as a producer of more than a half-dozen films. His TV shows dominated prime time with *All in the Family* (1971), winner of three Emmys, *Maude* (1972), *The Jeffersons* (1975), *Mary Hartman, Mary Hartman* (1976) and *The Baxters* (1979).

ANATOLE LITVAK (1902-74) b. Kiev, Russia
Director/Screenwriter He earned his credentials in European film making, notably for the French production of *Mayerling* (1936). His affiliation with Warner Brothers began soon after arriving in the U.S. He produced such hard-edged features as *City of Conquest* in 1940 and *Sorry, Wrong Number* in 1948. That same year he released his screen milestone *The Snake Pit*.

MARCUS LOEW (1870-1927) b. New York City
Motion Picture Executive One of the first to sense the potential of motion pictures, he partnered with Adolph Zukor in the penny arcade business, then branched out to establish the coast-to-coast chain of Loew Theaters. He also purchased Metro Pictures which merged in 1924 with the Goldwyn Company and Louis B. Mayer Pictures to create the Hollywood colossus, MGM.

ERNST LUBITSCH (1892-1947) b. Berlin, Germany
Director/Producer The artful wit and absurdities his movies introduced in the late 1920s added the phrase "the Lubitsch touch" to filmdom's lexicon. Among the most praised were *The Love Parade* (1929), *The Merry Widow* (1934), *Ninotchka* (1939) and others which previewed the talents of Mary Pickford, Jeanette MacDonald, Greta Garbo and Maurice Chevalier.

SIDNEY LUMET (1924-) b. Philadelphia, PA
Director/Screenwriter The luminary of stage and screen has offered audiences a pageant of sophisticated and thoughtful pictures. Among them are *Twelve Angry Men* (1957), *Long Day's Journey into Night* (1962), *The Pawnbroker* (1965), *Serpico* (1973) and *Network* (1976). In 1993 he received the D.W. Griffith Award from the Director' Guild, the organization's most coveted honor.

LOUIS B. MAYER   (1885-1957)   b. Minsk, Russia
Motion Picture Executive   The Hollywood film magnate was unmatched at organizing lucrative production companies. In 1917, he formed Louis B. Mayer Productions which later merged with Metro and Samuel Goldwyn. His organization retained directors Cecil B. DeMille and Irving Thalberg to lead the fledgling MGM into a key role in Hollywood's golden era.

DAVID MERRICK   (1912-)   b. St. Louis, MO
Theatrical Producer   A quarter-century of stage offerings by Broadway's producer for all seasons collected a record number of Tony nominations and awards. His conquest of the Great White Way began with *Fanny* (1954) followed by productions including *The Entertainer* (1958), *Gypsy* (1958), *Oliver* (1962), *Hello Dolly* (1964), *Sugar* (1972) and *Forty-Second Street* (1980).

JEROME MINSKOFF   (1916-94)   b. New York City
Impresario   The real estate attorney and developer became a contender for major Broadway productions when erecting the historic Minskoff Theater. It opened with a revival of *Irene* in 1973 and has since staged *Can-Can*, *Sweet Charity* and other major musicals. He also served as governor of the League of American Theaters and Producers.

MIKE NICHOLS   (1931-)   b. Berlin, Germany
Director/Producer   He enjoyed early success in improvisational comedy opposite Elaine May. Off on his own, he debuted on Broadway as the director of *Barefoot on the Park* (1963) and earned an Oscar as best director for *The Graduate* (1968). Other films adding to his screen credits include *Carnal Knowledge* (1971), *Regarding Henry* (1991) and *The Remains of the Day* (1993).

JOSEPH PAPP (1921-91) b. New York City
Director/Producer The theatrical innovator inaugurated the New York Shakespeare Festival and launched the off-Broadway Public Theater which staged the rock musical *Hair* (1967) and ever-popular *A Chorus Line* (1975). He won three Pulitzer Prizes, also raised funds to build his company's Delacorte theater in New York's Central Park and directed Lincoln Center's theaters.

ARTHUR PENN (1922-) b. Philadelphia, PA
Director/Screenwriter He began his career by directing two productions in rapid succession: the Broadway play *Two for the Seesaw* (1958) and *The Miracle Worker* (1960), a Tony Award winner which he filmed two years later. Known as an "actor's director" who drew fine performances from cast members, he received ten Oscar nominations for *Bonnie and Clyde* (1967).

SYDNEY POLLACK (1934-) b. Lafayette, IN
Director/Producer/Actor The Oscar-winning director of *Out of Africa* (1985) also earned awards and box office tribute for *They Shoot Horses, Don't They?* (1969), *The Way We Were* (1973) and *Tootsie* (1982). He also directed episodes of TV's *Ben Casey* serial before returning to acting in 1992 with performances in Robert Altman's *The Player* and Woody Allen's *Husbands and Wives*.

OTTO PREMINGER (1906-86) b. Vienna, Austria
Director/Producer Artful, erratic and productive, he left his trademark on more than forty films as an actor, director or producer. Praised abroad and on Broadway for his directorial skills with *Libel* (1935), he also led a crusade against motion picture censorship. His other films include *Laura* (1944), *The Moon is Blue* (1953) and *Porgy and Bess* (1959).

HAROLD PRINCE   (1928-)   b. New York City
Producer/Director He mounted some of Broadway's biggest hits and received sixteen Tonys for musicals including *Pajama Game* (1954), *Damn Yankees* (1955), *Fiorello!* (1959), *Fiddler on the Roof* (1964) and *Cabaret* (1966). During 26 years of stage success, he also launched *West Side Story* (1957), *Follies* (1971), *Sweeny Todd* (1979) and *Kiss of the Spider Woman* (1990).

SUMNER REDSTONE   (1923-)   b. Boston, MA
Entertainment Business Leader Since 1987, he headed Viacom International whose holdings in TV, movies, cable systems, publishing companies and amusement parks places it at the summit of the entertainment world. Viacom's MTV operations alone reach into eighty countries. He returned to his company's leadership role after recovering from near-fatal burns in 1979.

MAX REINHARDT   (1873-1943)   b. Baden, Austria
Director/Producer Originally schooled in stagecraft, he profoundly influenced the German motion picture industry with four impressionistic films. The mentor of young directors including Ernst Lubitsch also helped create the Marlene Dietrich mystique. Soon after his 1933 arrival in Hollywood, he filmed *A Midsummer Night's Dream*, adapted from his stage production.

JEROME ROBBINS   (1918-)   b. New York City
Choreographer The much-honored former dancer is best remembered for choreographing two productions of *West Side Story* (1957 and 1980) and *Fiddler on the Roof* (1964). In 1958 he formed his own company, Ballets U.S.A., and simultaneously created new programs for the New York City Ballet. His role in the evolution of American dance is evidenced on Broadway and in films.

BILLY ROSE (1899-1966) b. New York City
Showman/Impresario He began his career in the 1920s as a songwriter. Subsequently he acquired a string of night clubs including the famed Diamond Horseshoe and pioneered the practice of presenting showbiz celebrities on supper club stages. The Broadway producer and businessman was also an avid collector of art treasures, many of which were donated to museums.

GENE SAKS (1921-) b. New York City
Director His induction into the Theater Hall of Fame in 1991 honored a lifetime of stage and film work as a director and actor. Among the many plays he staged were Neil Simon's *Barefoot in the Park* (1963), *The Odd Couple* (1965) and *Broadway Bound*. He made his film directing debut with the screen adaptation of *Barefoot in the Park* in 1967.

JOHN SCHLESINGER (1926-) b. London, England
Director/Actor Feature films and documentaries produced in his homeland earned many international awards. Relocating to Hollywood, he directed *Midnight Cowboy*, a 1969 Oscar winner. The former actor has since completed films praised for their sensitivity and power: *Sunday, Bloody Sunday* (1971), *The Day of the Locust* (1975), *Marathon Man* (1976) and *The Believers* (1987).

DAVID O. SELZNICK (1902-65) b. Pittsburgh, PA
Producer The descendent of a film industry family began his career as a script reader at MGM and advanced to film making for Paramount and RKO. His faculty for coupling strong story lines with acting talent realized such sagas as *Rebecca* (1940), *David Copperfield* (1935), *Gone with the Wind* (1939), *Duel in the Sun* (1947), *Anna Karenina* (1948) and *A Farewell to Arms* (1957).

93

THE SHUBERTS (1870s-present) b. U.S.A.

Theater Owners/Producers The entrepreneurial family closely linked to theatricals owned and operated an estimated half of all America's opera houses and showplaces during the 1960s. The older brothers, Samuel, Lee and Jacob, also managed vaudeville and acting companies, and staged more than 500 productions featuring rising stars of the musical world.

FRED SILVERMAN (1937-) b. New York City

TV Producer/Executive For over two decades, he successfully programmed popular TV serials and specials for all three major networks. He formed his own company in 1982 and continued to produce and syndicate all-star TV series and films including *Perry Mason*, *Matlock*, *The Father Dowling Mysteries*, *The Time of Their Lives* and *In the Heat of the Night*.

AARON SPELLING (1928-) b. Dallas, TX

TV Producer/Writer He fed the public's appetite for action and sensuality with many of the medium's leading series and made-for-TV movies. *Charlie's Angels* (1976-81), *Fantasy Island* (1978-81), *Hart to Hart* (1979-84) and *Dynasty* (1981-89) were among them. An Emmy-winning documentary-style feature *Day One* (1989) presented the dramatic story of our entry into the atomic age.

STEVEN SPIELBERG (1947-) b. Cincinnati, OH

Director/Producer His devastating, Oscar-winning epic *Schindler's List* was completed the same year as *Jurassic Park* (1993) whose billion-dollar receipts made motion picture history. His other fantasy and sci-fi triumphs include *Jaws* (1975), *Close Encounters of the Third Kind* (1977), *Raiders of the Lost Ark* (1981), *E.T.* (1982) and the *Back to the Future* trilogy (1985, 89 and 90).

JULES STEIN (1896-1981) b. South Bend, IN
Entertainment Executive He left a prosperous practice in eye surgery to form the Music Corporation of America (1924). By the mid-1930s and 1940s, MCA represented almost half of the nation's top bands and Hollywood stars. Under his successor, MCA also acquired Universal Studios (1958), while he returned to medicine and founded a national eye research foundation.

OLIVER STONE (1946-) b. New York City
Director/Screenwriter The screenplay for *Midnight Express* (1978) produced his first Oscar, Writers Guild and Globe awards. A second Oscar was won for *Platoon* (1986), a graphic film about the Vietnamese war. A later film *Wall Street* (1987) excoriating financial industry corruption was followed by *JFK* (1991) theorizing a plot to assassinate the president.

LEE STRASBERG (1901-82) b. Budzanow, Austria
Acting Teacher/Director The instructor of Paul Newman, Marlon Brando, Marilyn Monroe and many others helped revolutionize the craft. He pioneered "method acting" derived from the Stanislavsky system which replaced histrionics with subtlety. His classes convened in The Group Theater he opened in New York (1931) and in its 1947 successor, the Actor's Studio.

ERICH von STROHEIM (1885-1957) b. Vienna, Austria
Director/Actor A temperamental professional, he reached high levels of realism and sophistication in the more than 45 films which he directed or in which he acted. These include *Greed* (1923), *The Merry Widow* (1925) and *Queen Kelly* (1928). He made his final U.S. screen appearance as the autocratic butler opposite Gloria Swanson in *Sunset Boulevard* (1950).

IRVING THALBERG (1899-1936) b. New York City
Producer Sixty years after his premature death, he is still regarded as "the boy wonder" whose pursuit of perfection produced the classics *The Hunchback of Notre Dame* (1923) and *Ben Hur* (1926). He revitalized film making at Universal and MGM, and led the industry into its era of sound. The Motion Picture Academy's prestigious Thalberg Award was established in his honor.

HARRY WARNER (1881-1958)

ALBERT WARNER (1883-1967)

SAMUEL WARNER (1887-1927)

JACK WARNER (1892-1978)
Producers The motion picture empire founded by the four Warner brothers was a resource for invention that helped Hollywood mature and grow through time. From its studios came ideas that laid the foundations of talking pictures, full-length features and color movies.

LEW WASSERMAN (1913-) b. Cleveland, OH
Motion Picture Executive He joined the Music Corporation of America (MCA) in 1936 and eventually rose to its executive leadership. As CEO, he piloted the conglomerate through troubled times into prosperity capped by the success of MCA's Universal Pictures. With philanthropic zeal, he also donated millions for eye research, scholarships and medical care programs.

WILLIAM WELLMAN (1896-1975) b. New York City
Director/Screenwriter The World War One fighter pilot and Croix de Guerre winner broke into Hollywood as an actor, then director. His movie *Wings* (1927) was the first to earn an Academy Award for best film, and *A Star is Born* (1937) netted him an Oscar

96

for screenplay. Other directorial hits include *Public Enemy* (1931), *The Ox Bow Incident* (1943) and *Battleground* (1949).

BILLY WILDER (1906-) b. Galicia, Poland
Director/Producer/Screenwriter He faithfully captured the dark landscape of American culture and values in films like *Double Indemnity* (1944), *The Lost Weekend* (1945) and *Sunset Boulevard* (1950). Seven Oscars were among many awards he won for writing and directing films of thematic variety, including *Some Like it Hot* (1959), *The Apartment* (1960) and *Buddy, Buddy* (1981).

FLORENZ ZIEGFELD (1869-1932) b. Chicago, IL
Theatrical Producer Since 1907 he staged 24 annual reviews, lavish spectaculars of great audience appeal. The *Ziegfeld Follies* were also prestigious showcases for rising stars, introducing the public to personalities like George Gershwin, Will Rogers, Eddie Cantor, Sigmund Romberg and Marilyn Miller. He also produced *Show Boat* (1927) and *Bitter Sweet* (1929).

ADOLPH ZUKOR (1873-1976) b. Rosce, Hungary
Motion Picture Executive The early giant of the film industry joined Marcus Loew in creating a network of penny arcades in 1903. Twelve years later, he formed Famous Players, a film company which became the Famous Players-Lasky Corporation. After acquiring Paramount, then of modest size, he linked with Samuel Goldwyn and C.B. DeMille in building it into a major studio.

Other Noted Directors, Producers and Executives

Irwin Allen – film producer

Steven H. Berman – TV executive

Arthur Cohn – film producer/distributor

Norman Corwin – radio, TV and film producer/director

Louis Edelman – film and TV producer

William Friedkin – film and TV director

Charles and **Daniel Frohman** – theatrical managers

Mark Goodson – TV producer

Sam Harris – theatrical producer

Stanley Jaffe – film producer/studio head

Howard W. Koch – film producer/director/playwright

Sherry Lansing – film producer/studio head

Joseph Levine – film producer

Joseph L. Mankewicz – film director/producer

Lee Mendelson – TV producer/writer

James Nederlander – theatrical producer

David Suskind – TV producer/program host

Ned Tanen – film producer/studio head

Irwin Winkler – film producer/director

Jerry Zacks – theatrical producer

Five
Scholarship and Education

In the impoverished villages of Eastern Europe, romanticized in *Fiddler on the Roof*, Jews created a rich and vibrant culture. Compensating for an outer life of hardship and struggle, ordinary people were swept by religious piety and mysticism that entered their music, poetry and storytelling.

Young men, venerated by their neighbors for their brilliance, might be financed in their studies with funds raised by townspeople. The dignity and prestige accorded to these intellectuals enhanced their chances for marriage into the "best" families.

On the other hand, German Jews in Western Europe were often members of an urban elite. Many were prosperous, sophisticated men of commerce and tradesmen who departed from orthodox ways. Others were politically active in unionism, and in economic and social reform movements. For some, education was a means of elevating their status among gentiles.

What bound the two culturally discrete groups during the emigrations of the 19th and 20th Centuries was a reverence for learning and knowledge.

They drifted into the swirl of America: poor immigrants in New York City's teeming Lower East Side, rich immigrants sometimes in palatial uptown homes. The two populations were isolated from one another by class and wealth, but seldom by intellect.

Many sons and daughters of immigrants from Eastern Europe were drawn to the life of the mind. They entered the intellectual community through schooling, often supported, as in the old country, by the earnings of relatives who invested hope in their young. For immigrant parents, the sweat shop was a workplace to fulfill a dream – a bequest to their young that would eventually bring pride and honor to their children and themselves.

The distinguished Jewish-American intellectuals, academics and philosophers who rose from that tradition did not disappoint their

99

parents and kinsmen. Even today, the collective I.Q. of these Americanized Jews and their offspring has been reported to compete with the highest found within other of the nation's ethnic and racial groups.

Scholars, Educators and Historians

CYRUS ADLER (1863-1940) b. Van Buren, AR
Educator The former Smithsonian Institution librarian organized many scientific and cultural organizations of Jewish interest. Included were the American Jewish Historical Society, American Jewish Committee and Jewish Welfare Board. He was editor of the *Jewish Quarterly Review* and president of Dropsie College (1908-40) and the Jewish Theological Seminary (1924-40).

FELIX ADLER (1851-1933) b. Alzey, Germany
Educator The teacher and social reformer founded the American Ethical Union in New York (1876), a nonsectarian movement which augments traditional religious beliefs with its philosophy of ethical humanism. As chairperson of the National Child Labor Committee, he helped liberalize laws affecting the young, and also originated the workshop concept of classroom teaching.

MORTIMER ADLER (1902-) b. New York City
Educator/Philosopher He left his professorship at Columbia University in 1929 to join the philosophy department of the University of Chicago. In that position he co-directed an ambitious enterprise – popularizing western civilization's cultural inheritance in the 54 volume set of *Great Books of the Western World* (1945-52). He also wrote philosophical essays.

HANNAH ARENDT (1906-75) b. Hanover, Germany
Political Scientist/Scholar As a political theorist and writer, the survivor of the Holocaust devoted much of her life to appraising institutional intolerance and racism. A ranking intellectual, she was the first woman to win a professorship at Princeton (1959). Her key study, *The Origins of Totalitarianism* (1951), was among the first to relate Communism to Nazism.

HAROLD BLOOM (1930-) b. New York City
Literary Scholar Considered a giant in his field, he has probed deeply into the romantic tradition of American and English poetry and has published assessments of the works of Percy Bysshe Shelley, William Blake, William Butler Yeats and Wallace Stevens. His *The Book of J* (1990) speculates that a female was one of four sources for the five books of the bible.

LEONARD BLOOMFIELD (1887-1949) b. Chicago, IL
Linguist A primary contribution to our scientific understanding of linguistics appears in his masterwork *Language* (1933) which is accepted today as a standard text. Its conclusion, that the spoken tongue is the only medium for analyzing language, was drawn from his studies of tribal languages of North America, Indo-European and other word origins.

DANIEL BOORSTIN (1914-) b. Atlanta, GA
Historian His writings on American history and civilization are admired for their scope, vision and authenticity. He is best known for *The Genius of American Politics* (1953), a trilogy titled *The Americans* (1958,65,73) and *The Discoverers* (1983). The University of Chicago professor (1944-69) was also director of the National Museum of History and Technology (1969-73).

NOAM CHOMSKY (1928-) b. Philadelphia, PA
Linguist The theories presented in *Syntactic Structures* (1957) and other works by the MIT professor overthrew beliefs that language skills are entirely acquired. His premise, that language structure is partly inborn and intuitive, further advanced in *Language and Mind* (1968) and *Reflections on Language* (1976), is today supported by the world's philologists and psychologists.

JOSEPH EPSTEIN (1937-) b. New York City
Essayist The prolific essayist has written extensively about attitudes and behaviors of Americans under social stress. *Divorced in America: Marriage in an Age of Possibility* (1974) and *Familiar Territory: Observations on American Life* (1979) have been well received. His recent *Partial Payments: Essays Arising From the Pleasures of Reading* (1989) is personal and reflective.

LESLIE FIEDLER (1917-) b. Newark, NJ
Critic/Author Novelist, essayist, poet, professor and literary critic, he has written incisive works including *Image of the Jew in American Fiction* (1959) and *Love and Death in the American Novel* (1966). He presumes that the unconscious sexual urges of authors frequently inform their writings, a viewpoint that has deepened our understanding of the creative process.

ABRAHAM FLEXNER (1866-1959) b. Louisville, KY
Educator The strength and character of modern medical education and training in North America owes much to an activist scholar who exhaustively studied the procedures of medical schools and proposed reforms. He was equally involved in evaluating secondary and higher institutions of learning, and founded the celebrated Institute for Advanced Study in Princeton, NJ.

JAMES FREEDMAN (1936-) b. Manchester, NH
College President He assumed the presidency of Dartmouth College after distinguished careers as president of the University of Iowa and dean of the University of Pennsylvania Law School. His advice for fulfilling the duties of an educator is summed up an often-quoted remark: "to act with judicious tolerance and apply the quiet, measured force of reason."

BETTY FRIEDAN (1921-) b. Peoria, IL
Feminist Author The feminist writer and liberationist is best known for *The Feminine Mystique* (1963) which sounded a call for women's equality in American and global society. She was a founder of the National Organization for Women (NOW) in 1966 and is a persistent crusader against sexual discrimination. A sequel published in 1981, titled *The Second Stage*, extends her message.

NATHAN GLAZER (1923-) b. New York City
Sociologist He first came to public attention as an observer of urban social behavior in *The Lonely Crowd* (1950), co-authored with David Riesman. The respected educator, lecturer and essayist also wrote *American Judaism* (1957), *Beyond the Melting Pot* (1963) in collaboration with Senator Daniel Patrick Moynihan, and *The Public Interest on Crime and Punishment* (1984).

OSCAR HANDLIN (1915-) b. New York City
Historian A Harvard professor and student of America's cultural and economic evolution, he shed new light on the influences of emigration on society, the economic basis of slavery and politics in a democratic state. Among his books are *The Uprooted* (1951 Pulitzer Prize) and *The Americans* (1963). He also directed the Center for the Study of Liberty (1958-66).

IRVING HOWE (1920-93) b. New York City
Critic/Editor/Essayist The founder and long-term editor of *Dissent* magazine (1953) espoused and debated the theory of democratic socialism. *World of Our Fathers* earned him a National Book Award in 1976. He also wrote critical studies of famous authors. *A Critic's Notebook*, published after his death, is a tribute to the art of fiction.

JUSTIN KAPLAN (1925-) b. New York City
Biographer/Essayist A distinguished biographer, he has lectured at Harvard University and is currently on the faculty of the College of the Holy Cross. His major works include *Mr. Clemens and Mark Twain* (1966), *Lincoln Steffens: A Biography* (1974) and *Mark Twain and His World* (1974). More recently, he produced a definitive biography of poet Walt Whitman (1980).

ALFRED KAZIN (1915-95) b. New York City
Critic/Author A professor and lecturer at leading universities, he authored studies of American literature, as well as articles and reviews. *On Native Grounds* (1942), his interpretation of modern American literature, was followed by appraisals of Melville, Dreiser, Fitzgerald and Emerson. His several autobiographies included *A Walker in the City* (1951).

JOSEPH LASH (1909-87) b. New York City
Historian/Biographer He was better known outside of academic circles as the biographer of Eleanor Roosevelt's mature years which he developed in two volumes titled *Eleanor and Franklin* (1971 Pulitzer Prize) and *Eleanor, the Years Alone* (1972). His other biographies of Helen Keller and Dag Hammarskjold were also praised.

104

MICHAEL LERNER (1943-) b. Newark, NJ
Political Philosopher The standard bearer for "the politics of meaning" has promoted a philosophy endorsing social responsibility and unselfishness as social goals, a principle adopted by the Clinton administration to justify proposed policy. A social activist with two Ph.D.s from the University of California, he edits *Tikkun*, an independent journal of opinion.

GEORGE JEAN NATHAN (1882-1958) b. Fort Wayne, IN
Drama Critic/Editor The theater critic for *Harpers Weekly* (1908-10) joined H.L. Mencken as editors of the *Smart Set* (1914-23). Together they founded *The American Mercury* with which he was associated until 1941. The peppery and contentious articles of a ranking critic of his day influenced playwrights Eugene O'Neill, Arthur Miller and William Saroyan.

MENACHEM SCHNEERSON (1902-94) b. Nikolaev, Russia
Spiritual Leader Honoring his memory as the inspiring head of a worldwide Hasidic sect, the nation posthumously awarded the Lubavitch rabbi a 1995 Congressional Gold Medal. He was esteemed by many as this generation's greatest Jewish thinker, a personage of powerful logic and intellect. His teachings urged a moral foundation for all of life's endeavors.

SUSAN SONTAG (1933-) b. New York City
Essayist/Critic A prestigious literary figure with degrees from the University of Chicago and Harvard, she holds nonconformist views on politics and freedom of expression. Her positions have been assailed by both sides of the political and intellectual spectrum. The widely published essayist wrote an account of her near-fatal ailment in the much praised *Illness as Metaphor* (1978).

105

ALVIN TOFFLER   (1928-)   b. New York City
Futurist His bestseller *Future Shock* (1970) raised a premise for which he was labeled as both an alarmist and a prophet – that technological advances have outstripped society's ability to absorb them, leading to psychological overload. In its sequel *The Third Wave* (1980) he presented ideas for modifying technology's negative impacts on human development.

LIONEL TRILLING   (1905-75)   b. New York City
Critic/Educator/Essayist A literary eminence, he taught and lectured at major universities, including Harvard and Oxford, and was a contributor to leading intellectual journals. Among his best known writings and collections of essays were *Matthew Arnold* (1939), *The Middle of the Journey* (1947), *The Liberal Imagination* (1950) and *Beyond Culture* (1965).

BARBARA TUCHMAN   (1912-89)   b. New York City
Historian Clarity, scope and analysis were attributes of one of the most widely read and esteemed historians of her generation. She twice won Pulitzer Prizes: for her volume on World War One *The Guns of August* in 1963 and for *Stillwell and the American Experience in China* in 1972. She was the first female president of the American Institute of Arts and Letters (1979).

JEROME WIESNER   (1915-94)   b. Dearborn, MI
College President/Scientist The productive author and science advisor to President John F. Kennedy served from 1971-80 as president of the Massachusetts Institute of Technology. A graduate electrical engineer, he had contributed to radar technology early in his career. He also designed electronic components for atomic bomb testing while at Los Alamos.

Other Noted Scholars, Educators and Historians

Daniel Bell
- university professor and leading social critic

Allan Bloom
- author of *The Closing of the American Mind*

Leon Botstein
- president of Bard College, NY

Harold Brown
- president of California Institute of Technology

Phyllis Chesler
- psychologist and feminist theorist

Arthur Cohen
- scholar of fiction, nonfiction and philosophy

Lawrence Cremin
- president of Columbia's Teachers College

Ariel Durant
- co-author with husband Will of world histories

Leon Edel
- Pulitzer Prize-winning biographer

Joseph Epstein
- editor of the *American Scholar*

Edward Epstein
- respected critic of the network media

James Freedman
- president of Dartmouth College

Alexander Goldenweiser
- foremost expert on American Indian lore

Eric Goldman
- historian and presidential consultant

Samuel Gould
- president of New York University

Louis Harris
- pollster and social analyst

Henry Harrisse
- founded the modern school of historical research

Isaac Hays
- past secretary, American Philosophical Society

Gertrude Himmelfarb
- promotes Victorian values for social health

David Horowitz
- founder, Center for the Study of Popular Culture

Jane Jacobs
- commentator and critic on cities and urban planning

Morris Janowitz
- analyst of the social impacts of technology

Alfred Kahn
- social planner for agencies and foundations

Horace Kallen
- leading exponent of "cultural pluralism"

Herbert Kohl
- advocate for the "open classroom" concept

Jonathan Kozol
- educational writer and critic

Herbert Leibowitz
- scholar, editor, *Parnassus: Poetry in Review*

Edward Levi
- president of the University of Chicago

Richard Levin
- president of Yale University

Edward Luttwak
– military historian and analyst

Herbert Marcuse
– philosopher who popularized Marxist "humanism"

Martin Mayer
– critic of American school system and economy

Annie Meyer
– pioneering founder of Barnard College for women

Ernst Nagel
– advanced theories for systematizing knowledge

Max Neuburger
– noted scholar of ancient and medieval medicine

Robert Nozick
– philosopher, advocate for limited federal power

Marcus Raskin
– co-founder of the Institute for Policy Studies

Diane Ravitch
– author, *National Standards in American Education*

David Riesman
– sociologist and author of *The Lonely Crowd*

David Rothenberg
– prison reformer and criminology expert

Abram Sachar
– first president of Brandeis University

Peter Schrag
– social critic, author of *Decline of the WASP*

Gilbert Seldes
– critic and author of *The Seven Lively Arts*

Meyer Schapiro
– art historian and Columbia professor

Charles Silberman
- sociologist author of *Crisis in the Classroom*

Michael Sovern
- president of Columbia University

Ronald Steel
- author of *Walter Lippman and the American Century*

William Stern
- author of *Psychology of Early Childhood*

Leo Strauss
- philosophical godfather of neo-conservatism

Howard Taubman
- influential music critic for *The New York Times*

Calvin Trillin
- widely published humorous essayist, satirist

Diana Trilling
- essayist, critic, wife of Lionel Trilling

Michael Walzer
- sociologist, author of *Just and Unjust Wars*

Daniel Yankelovich
- pollster and professor of psychology

Harry Zimmerman
- founder of Albert Einstein College of Medicine

Howard Zinn
- author of *A People's History of the United States*

Paul Zweig
- cultural historian, literary critic, Whitman scholar

Six
Journalism, Communications and Publishing

Jews have been associated with the American news and entertainment media in impressive numbers – in book publishing, radio, television and the press. All three of our country's major radio and TV networks were launched or managed by Jewish executives. America's newspaper of record, *The New York Times*, and the influential *Washington Post* claim Jewish ownerships. Given their needs and values, the Jews' prominence in the world of information would seem inevitable.

Reaching into the minds and hearts of the Jewish community, Abraham Cahan, a Russian immigrant, established the *Daily Forward* in 1897. The first Yiddish paper of professional quality and content dominated its field and enjoyed a peak circulation of 100,000. It helped mold the attitudes of a readership coming to terms with a new and bewildering culture.

By 1905 the Jewish population of Greater New York approached one-million as waves of newcomers swelled its numbers. Both the well educated and less sophisticated hungered for information about their new homeland. Other Jewish language journals appeared and joined to help Jews seek out and fill their niche in American society.

As the Yiddish media matured, it became much more than a news conduit for the community. In a transition to larger ideals and purposes, publishers and journalists ventured into the national scene. Not necessarily as propagandists for Jewish interests, but as seasoned communicators who recognized a huge market for information.

As the technology of electronic transmission advanced, media pioneers sensed a promise to amass vast audiences. Among them were David Sarnoff who formed NBC in 1926, William Paley

111

of CBS, and Leonard Goldenson of ABC who helped power the authority and outreach of radio, then television, to new heights.

By their presence in publishing houses, newspaper offices and TV studios, Jews continue to prove that a climate of liberty nurtures their enterprise and talents as communicators. An instrument of democracy – freedom of speech – has been their lever for reaffirming and protecting the American way of life.

Journalists, Correspondents and Columnists

JOYCE BROTHERS   (1927-)   b. New York City
Columnist/TV Personality She was among the first psychologists to gain national prominence via the mass media. The former columnist for *Good Housekeeping* had hosted several call-in shows: *Consult Dr. Brothers* (1960-66) and *Ask Dr. Brothers* (1965-75). A prolific author of self-help psychology books, she has produced bestsellers including *What Every Woman Should Know About Men* (1982).

ART BUCHWALD   (1925-)   b. Mt. Vernon, NY
Humor Columnist He has authored satirical columns that were syndicated in U.S. newspapers and *The Paris Herald Tribune* for more than a half century. His targets are often government blunders and social conventions. He won a Pulitzer Prize for Commentary (1982), published more than twenty books and was elected to the American Academy of Arts and Sciences.

DAN DORFMAN   (1932-)
Financial Reporter During his forty years in business journalism and TV reportage, he delivered financial forecasts on CNN's *Moneyline* and more recently became a stock analyst on CNBC's *The Dorfman Report*. His bylined columns have appeared in *USA*

Today and *The Wall Street Journal*. He currently bylines a financial column for *Money* magazine.

THOMAS LOREN FRIEDMAN (1953-) b. Minneapolis, MN
Journalist/Columnist The newsman worked his way up through the ranks of *The New York Times*, from chief economic and White House correspondent to Op-Ed page columnist on foreign affairs. While a bureau chief in Lebanon and Israel, he earned Pulitzer Prizes for reportage in 1983 and 1988. His *From Beirut to Jerusalem* won a 1989 National Book Award for non-fiction.

ELLEN HOLTZ GOODMAN (1941-) b. Newton, MA
Columnist/News Commentator Her journalistic posts included feature writer and columnist for the *Boston Globe* (1967-74) which named her associate editor in 1986. Concurrently, she wrote for *The Washington Post Writers Group*, *Newsweek* and authored five books. She served as a commentator on *CBS Spectrum* and on NBC's *Today Show*, and won a Pulitzer Prize for Commentary in 1980.

JOSEPH KRAFT (1924-86) b. South Orange, NJ
Columnist The syndicated Washington journalist and three-time winner of Overseas Press Club Awards for distinguished reporting (1958,73,80) also received Columbia University's John Jay Award for Distinguished Professional Achievement (1983). His column appeared in *The Los Angeles Times*, *The Washington Post* and in 200 other newspapers in the U.S. and overseas.

ANN LANDERS (1918-) b. Sioux City, Iowa
Personal Advice Columnist "Ask Ann Landers" debuted as a daily feature in 1955 and currently appears in more than 1,200 newspapers. An average 2,000 letters arrive at her *Chicago Trib-*

une offices each day, accounting for her reputation as the world's most widely syndicated columnist. She crafts wit and sound counsel into every answer published in her columns.

MAX LERNER (1902-92) b. Minsk, Russia
Political Columnist The commentator on American politics and values shared his views in college classrooms and through a syndicated column. His articles frequently appeared in magazines including *Atlantic Monthly, Saturday Review* and *The New Republic*. Among his most provocative books were *Ideas Are Weapons* (1939) and *The Age of Overkill* (1962).

WALTER LIPPMAN (1889-1974) b. New York City
Journalist/Columnist The social observer, philosopher and commentator left the editorial desk of the *New York World* in 1931 for the *New York Herald Tribune*. There he wrote a daily political column that gained an international readership and a 1962 Pulitzer Prize. His books include *A Preface to Politics* (1913), *The Cold War* (1947) and *The Public Philosophy* (1955).

SYLVIA PORTER (1913-91) b. Long Island, NY
Financial Columnist More than twenty-five million American readers consulted her financial column which appeared three-times weekly in 430 newspapers around the world. She also published several informative self-help books commended by economic and financial experts. Her first bestseller *Sylvia Porter's Money Book* (1975) sold more than three million copies.

WILLIAM SAFIRE (1929-) b. New York City
Columnist The former speech writer for President Nixon and Vice President Agnew is today a protagonist of conservative political writing in *The New York Times*. His journalistic investigation of

the Burt Lance financial scandal won a Pulitzer Prize in 1978. He also writes a weekly column, "On Language," which whimsically analyzes the origins and usage of English words and phrases.

LEONARD SILK (1918-95) b. Philadelphia, PA
Columnist For decades, *Business Week* and *The New York Times* published his views on complex economic and business issues translated into layman's language. One of the few American reporters with a Ph.D., he had authored fifteen books on the forces affecting the state of the nation. Typically: *Nixonomics* (1972) and *Capitalism: the Moving Target* (1973).

HERBERT BAYARD SWOPE (1882-1958) b. St. Louis, MO
Journalist Inside the German Empire, his collection of World War One news stories published in 1917, won the first Pulitzer Prize for reportage. Other honors came to the flamboyant newsman from *The New York World* whose investigative reporting of crime and the Ku Klux Klan set benchmarks for U.S. journalism. In later years he consulted for various federal agencies.

THEODORE WHITE (1915-86) b. Boston, MA
Journalist/Author Cited for his "brilliant presentation of democracy in action," the Pulitzer Prize-winning writer was best known for his now-classic books examining electoral politics and the presidency: *The Making of the President* (1960, 64, 68, 72). His myriad writings probed the political, cultural and social sweep of our nation with sensitivity, candor and humor.

WALTER WINCHELL (1897-1972) b. New York City
Columnist The powerful gossip columnist and broadcaster was called an architect of modern tabloid journalism. His savage opinions and abrasive style drew two-thirds of America's weekly

readers and radio listeners. Often lashing out at socialites and politicians, he was also among the first newsmen to strongly denounce the rise of Nazism in Germany.

Other Noted Journalists, Correspondents and Columnists

Cindi Adams
–syndicated show business columnist

Carl Bernstein
– *Washington Post* reporter who exposed Watergate

Eric Breindel
– editorial page editor of the *New York Post*

David Broder
– Pulitzer Prize-winning *Washington Post* columnist

Judith Christ
– nationally syndicated film reviewer

Don Feder
– editorial writer and columnist for *The Boston Herald*

Max Frankel
– news columnist for *The New York Times*

Arthur Gelb
– news editor and writer for *The New York Times*

Paul Goldberger
– art editor and writer for *The New York Times*

Ellen Goodman
– columnist and news reporter

Nat Hentoff
– critic and columnist focusing on jazz

Seymour Hersh
– Pulitzer Prize-winning investigative journalist

Pauline Kael
 – nationally syndicated movie reviewer

Stanley Kauffman
 – film and theater critic for *The New Republic*

Marvin Kitman
 – nationally syndicated columnist

Arthur Krock
 – *New York Times* columnist and bureau chief

Irv Kupcinet
 – news columnist and reporter

Irving R. Levine
 – economics editor of NBC TV News

Anthony Lewis
 – news columnist for *The New York Times*

Flora Lewis
 – reporter on international politics

Leonard Lyons
 – show business and celebrity columnist

Herbert Mitgang
 – cultural correspondent and journalist

Jack Newfield
 – investigative reporter and political columnist

A.H. Raskin
 – labor reporter

Frank Rich
 – film, theater and cultural columnist

A.M. Rosenthal
 – executive editor/columnist, *The New York Times*

Sydney Shanberg
 – journalist, author of *The Killing Fields*

Lisa Shiffren
– columnist for the *American Spectator*

John Simon
– film and theater reviewer and columnist

I.F. Stone
– investigative journalist and newsletter editor

Tad Szulc
– news reporter and author

Abigail Van Buren
– syndicated personal advice columnist

TV/Radio Correspondents and Commentators

LARRY KING (1933-) b. New York City

Talk Show Host His career was launched in 1957 behind a broom, while sweeping the floors of an obscure 250-watt AM station in Florida. Today he is a superstar interviewer whose *Larry King Live* show is beamed nightly over CNN, and whose radio show is heard by 3.5 million listeners. National and world leaders often bid for preview appearances before his studio cameras.

EDWIN NEWMAN (1919-) b. New York City

TV Commentator/Journalist The reporter once scripted stories for CBS evening news in Washington D.C. (1947-49). He left for assignments as an NBC News correspondent in London, Rome, Paris and in New York City where his commentary was telecast since 1961. He has written for King Features Syndicate and authored *Strictly Speaking* (1974) and other books on English usage.

LAWRENCE SPIVAK (1901-94) b. New York City
TV News Show Host Today's confrontational TV programs, facing off newsmen with guests, owe their inspiration to his ground breaking *Meet the Press*, the medium's longest running series. His persistent and perceptive style of inquiry set a pattern other hosts have adopted. A number of momentous news breaks were announced or leaked on his program by world leaders.

MIKE WALLACE (1918-) b. Brookline, MA
TV Journalist The ageless co-anchor of the CBS news magazine *60 Minutes* and winner of ten Emmy Awards is a ground breaker for TV's investigative journalism. His rise to television stardom began with his on-site 1962 coverage of America's early involvement in the Vietnam war and during the decade that followed. He is known for his probing, no-nonsense interview style.

BARBARA WALTERS (1931-) b. Boston, MA
TV Journalist The current co-host of *20/20* had become a prominent TV personality through interviews held with world leaders and celebrities on news programs and specials. The many honors she has won during decades of reportage include Emmy and Peabody awards. Gallup polls conducted in 1981 and 1984 named her one of America's most admired people.

RUTH WESTHEIMER (1928-) b. Frankfort, Germany
Sex Advisor Her first radio show *Sexually Speaking* (1980) aired weekly broadcasts by America's most enthusiastic spokesperson for uninhibited, guilt-free sexual lifestyles. Dr. Ruth has since been hailed as "our first true superstar sex therapist." Her visibility on national TV and radio is augmented with bestsellers including *First Love* (1985) and *The Art of Arousal* (1993).

Other Noted TV/Radio Correspondents and Commentators

Martin Agronsky
– international news and political commentator

Shana Alexander
– interviewer and news show host

Elizabeth Drew
– political commentator and writer

Henry Grunwald
– editor-in-chief of Time, Inc.

Bernard Kalb
– news correspondent and author

Marvin Kalb
– journalist and foreign correspondent

Ted Koppel
– host and interviewer on TV's *Nightline*

Jeffrey Lyons
– motion picture and theater reviewer

Michael Medved
– TV and newspaper film reviewer

Roger Rosenblatt
– TV and newspaper commentator and essayist

Lynn Scher
– TV host and news reporter

David Schoenbrun
– TV news commentator and essayist

Daniel Schorr
– won three Emmys for his Watergate news coverage

Gene Shalit
– motion picture reviewer and columnist

Joel Siegel
– motion picture reviewer

Murray Shiskal
 – motion picture reviewer

Leslie Stahl
 – co-anchor and interviewer for TV's *60 Minutes*

Howard Stern
 – earthy, controversial morning radio personality

Publishers, Editors, Executives and Producers

JULIUS OCHS ADLER (1892-1955) b. Chattanooga, TN
Newspaper Executive The former owner of *The Chattanooga Times* and first vice president of *The New York Times* twice interrupted his career as journalist and management executive to serve in both World Wars. He commanded the 77th Infantry Division in the Pacific as a brigadier general, and returned to pilot the paper published by his uncle, Adolph Ochs.

WALTER ANNENBERG (1908-) b. Milwaukee, WI
Publisher The self-made billionaire and friend of Presidents and royalty transformed his father's failing Triangle Publications into a communications empire. Triangle gained huge readerships with properties including *Seventeen Magazine* and *TV Guide*. He served as ambassador to England in 1968 and gave millions to the Annenberg Foundation and a school of communications.

BENNETT CERF (1898-1971) b. New York City
Publisher/Humorist Under his leadership since 1927, Random House rapidly expanded operations and became one of America's largest, most venerated publishers. During a fifteen-year parallel career on radio and TV, he was a panelist on *What's My Line?* He also edited anthologies of short stories, including *The Encyclopedia of Modern American Humor* (1954).

FRED FRIENDLY (1915-) b. New York City
TV Producer/Journalist Ten Peabody awards support his reputation as the conscience of news broadcasting. A past president of CBS news (1964-66) and advisor on TV for the Ford Foundation, he has produced numerous seminars on PBS examining ethical issues in news gathering and reporting. His latest of six books is *The Presidency and the Constitution* (1987).

HARRY GOLDEN (1902-1981) b. New York City
Editor/Humorist From 1941 to 1968, his national newspaper, *The Carolina Israelite*, was a platform for scornful humor aimed at segregation and bigotry, and for outspoken support of civil rights causes. He frequently took his crusade on lecture tours. Many of his anecdotal articles appeared in his first bestseller *Only in America* (1958) and in its sequels.

LEONARD GOLDENSON (1905-) b. Scottsdale, PA
TV Executive The CEO of United Paramount Theaters merged his company with ABC in 1953, creating the American Broadcasting Company in a move that challenged NBC and CBS for network leadership. He pioneered programming concepts that established TV as a primary medium of mass communication.

KATHERINE GRAHAM (1917-) b. New York City
Publisher The daughter of financier Eugene Meyer took control of *The Washington Post, Newsweek* magazine and a number of TV stations after the death of her publisher husband in 1963. Under her management, the *Post* excelled in exposing wrongdoing in high places in government – the Watergate conspiracy among them. She relinquished its presidency to her son Donald in 1979.

ALFRED A. KNOPF (1892-1984) b. New York City
Publisher Soon after its formation in 1915 by the 23-year old visionary, Alfred A. Knopf Inc. flexed its literary muscle. The house met success with *Green Mansions* and began issuing the works of famous foreign writers. Its authors have included Somerset Maughm, E.M. Forster and Sigmund Freud – writers who led the field in bringing Nobel Prizes home to their publisher.

WILLIAM LEONARD (1916-94)
TV News Executive The president of CBS News (1974-82) originated TV's highly popular news formats: magazine-style programming such as *60 Minutes* and the exit-poll technique for projecting election results. Beforehand, he completed a fifteen-year assignment as host of *Eye on New York*. He also hosted and produced a number of well-received TV documentaries.

LEO LERMAN (1914-94) b. New York City
Editor/Author He began his lifetime career as a writer and editor after leaving the theater as an actor and stage manager. Joining Condé Nast magazines, he won recognition for articles on theater and the arts, and as an editor with *Vogue* and *Mademoiselle*. He also served as editor-in-chief of *Vanity Fair* (1983) during his half-century with the publisher.

HORACE LIVERIGHT (1886-1933) b. Osceola Mills, PA
Publisher He was responsible for launching the *Modern Library*, an American literary treasure. In addition, the promotion-minded publisher of classics brought many fledgling and established novelists and poets to readers: Sherwood Anderson, William Faulkner, Ernest Hemingway and Ezra Pound to name a few. He was also a successful theatrical producer.

123

EUGENE MEYER (1857-1959) b. Los Angeles, CA
Publisher The former investment banker served as a governor of the Federal Reserve Board under President Hoover, and chaired FDR's Reconstruction Finance Corporation. He bought and resurrected the failing *Washington Post* in 1933, then acquired *Newsweek* magazine and several radio stations. Harry S. Truman later named him the first president of the World Bank in 1946.

ADOLPH OCHS (1858-1935) b. Cincinnati, OH
Publisher A printer's apprentice by early trade, he took control of *The Chattanooga Times* in 1896. After eighteen years, he relocated north and purchased *The New York Times* which was then on the brink of bankruptcy. He coined the memorable slogan, "All the news that's fit to print" for the paper as it grew into a world-class daily of prestige and power.

WILLIAM PALEY (1901-90) b. Chicago, IL
Media Executive Upon assuming the leadership of CBS, he organized sixteen faltering radio stations into a system that evolved into a major TV network. During a long reign at CBS, he retained such personalities as Edward R. Murrow, Bing Crosby and Jack Benny. He developed a news policy stressing integrity and elevated the status of television in news broadcasting.

NORMAN PEARLSTINE (1943-) b. Philadelphia, PA
Editor Four Pulitzer Prizes were won by the *Wall Street Journal* during the years it prospered under his editorial authority (1986-92). His creativity and leadership skills are currently at work at the Time Warner family of seven magazines which he heads as editor-in-chief. His resposibilities include *Time, Sports Illustrated, People* and *Money* magazine.

124

NORMAN PODHORETZ (1930-) b. New York City
Editor/Author Under his direction since 1960, the Jewish intellectual monthly *Commentary* has become a premier medium for
earnest social and political debate. He is also a literary critic and
author of an autobiography *Making It* (1967) and its sequel *Breaking Ranks* (1979). His political shift to neo-conservatism has
influenced much of his recent writings.

JOSEPH PULITZER (1847-1911) b. Mako, Hungary
Publisher/Editor The Civil War Union Army veteran advanced
from reporter to newspaper magnate when he founded *The St.
Louis Post-Dispatch* (1878) to which he added *The New York
World* (1883) and *The Evening World* (1887). His papers thrived
on sensationalism and pro-labor sympathy. He later endowed
Columbia University's School of Journalism (1903) and the Pul-
itzer Prizes.

DAVID SARNOFF (1891-1971) b. Uzlian, Russia
Media Executive His bold leadership contributed to the growth
of radio and television as premier vehicles for communication.
While president of the Radio Corporation of America, he formed
the National Broadcasting Company as an RCA subsidiary (1926).
"The father of American television" raised RCA's stake in color
TV and built the company into a giant in its field.

DOROTHY SCHIFF (1903-) b. New York City
Publisher/Editor The daughter of financier Jacob Schiff gained
control of *The New York Post* in 1941, and as editor and publisher
led the resurgence of America's oldest continuously published
evening newspaper. She was among the first women of her time
to manage a major daily, and was also committed to promoting
child welfare and health care programs serving New York City.

MAX SCHUSTER (1897-1970) b. Austria
Publisher The co-founder of Simon and Schuster (1924), and man of letters, was a pioneer in mass marketing quality titles through several of his company's divisions. His first-of-its-kind offerings in the U.S. were *Pocket Book* paperbacks, followed by the *Little Golden Books* series designed and illustrated for very young readers. He also edited literary anthologies.

WILLIAM SHAWN (1907-92) b. Chicago, IL
Editor He was eulogized by those who knew him as the greatest magazine editor who ever lived, and one of the period's most important American men of letters. The spirit and personality behind *The New Yorker* for 35 years received such accolades from the writers he cultivated: Dorothy Parker, Robert Benchley, Truman Capote, J.D. Salinger, Rachel Carson and John Hersey.

GLORIA STEINEM (1934-) b. Toledo, OH
Editor/Author The freelance writer with a Phi Beta Kappa once worked as a Playboy Bunny to research an article on sexism and women's status. Similar feminist concerns led her to co-found *Ms.* magazine in 1972. The author of four books also helped institute the Women's Action Alliance, the Coalition for Labor Union Women, and the National Women's Political Caucus.

ARTHUR OCHS SULZBERGER (1926-) b. Mt. Kisco, NY
Publisher Under his chairmanship (1973-92), *The New York Times* became the most widely consulted and quoted newspaper in the world. National and international leaders and policy makers have relied on its reportage guided by the objectivity, restraint and integrity of an award-winning staff of journalists and writers.

JAMES WECHSLER (1915-83) b. New York City
Editor/Author His column in *The New York Post* was among the first and most intrepid in challenging the excesses of Senator Joseph McCarthy. After filling the editor's seat, he steered the paper on a liberal course until 1976 when it took a conservative tilt. His books included *Revolt on Campus* (1935) and *Labor Baron* (1944), an autobiography of John L. Lewis.

Other Noted Publishers and Editors

Adam Bellow
– editorial director of *The Free Press*

Martin Peretz
– editor-in-chief of *The New Republic*

Letty Pogrebin
– co-founder and former editor of *Ms.* magazine

Joel Spingarn
– publisher and a founder/president of the NAACP

Mort Zuckerman
– publisher of the *U.S. News & World Report*

Syndicated Comics and Political Cartoonists

Herbert Block (Herblock)
– Pulitzer-winning political cartoonist

Al Capp
– *Li'l Abner* comic strip

Milton Coniff
– *Terry and the Pirates* comic strip

127

Max Fleischer
- *Betty Boop* comic strip

Isadore "Fritz" Freleng
- creator of Bugs Bunny, Daffy Duck, Porky Pig, Tweety Pie, Speedy Gonzalez and the Pink Panther animated cartoon characters

Reuben "Rube" Goldberg
- illustrator of incredibly ingenious machines to perform simple or purposeless tasks, appearing in hundreds of newspapers, and winner of a 1948 Pulitzer Prize for political cartooning

Harry Hershfield
- *Ish Kabibble* comic strip

Bob Kane
- *Batman* comic strip

Stan Lee
- *Spiderman* and *The Hulk* comic strips

Jerry Siegel and Joe Shuster
- *Superman* comic strip

Seven
Government, Law and the Military

At the turn of the century, New York, Boston, Philadelphia and Baltimore were being transformed by ambitious and energetic immigrants. Manhattan and its boroughs became bustling hubs of manufacturing and commercial activity. American urban centers, as well as smaller cities and towns, required political and civic institutions to serve their communities. Attorneys, judges and political officials were needed, but were in short supply.

Many educated Jewish-Americans entered the fields of law, politics and government. Living in a democracy ruled by law was new to their families' experience, and they responded by claiming a stake in their country's future and promise.

The practice of law, as a springboard to judicial and legislative office, was a magnet for many, and America's legal system has been well served by their contributions. Benjamin Cardozo, Louis Brandeis, Felix Frankfurter and Arthur Goldberg were among the outstanding Jews appointed to the U.S. Supreme Court.

Contributions have also been made at the highest echelons of government by Jewish diplomats, political scientists and statesmen. Bernard Baruch, the advisor to the Presidents, and Henry Kissinger, the Nobel Prize-winning Secretary of State, were among the most illustrious.

Public service had absorbed Jews in other countries as well. Benjamin Disraeli, the 19th Century English prime minister, was but one head of government of Jewish descent. During this century, thirteen others had been elected or appointed chiefs of state of eight nations.

Since our country's founding, America's armed forces were indebted to the patriotism of Jews who fought and died in our country's wars, and American Jews were early in combat. Example: while master of the warship, *Argus*, during the War of 1812,

Commodore Uriah Levy sank 21 British vessels and later proposed the law that ended flogging in the U.S. Navy.

More than 7,000 Jews served in the Civil War, nine of whom held the rank of general. Major General Maurice Rose, killed in action while commanding the 3rd Armored Division in Europe, was a much decorated hero of World War Two. More than 62,000 Jewish military personnel – among the quarter-million under arms – were also casualties of that war. And Admiral Hyman Rickover, father of the atomic submarine, became a prominent figure in U.S. military history.

Jews have aspired to living dutiful, ethical and patriotic lives in partnership with its government and institutions. Like a beacon, these principles of service have guided the Jew's 350 year odyssey on American soil.

People in Government

MORRIS ABRAM   (1918-)   b. Fitzgerald, GA

Public Official   The attorney by profession was also an intelligence officer with the U.S. Air Force during World War Two, and later officiated at the Nuremberg war crimes trials. Several appointments followed his release from service: as a counsel for the Marshall Plan and as JFK's first counsel for the Peace Corps. He assumed the presidency of Brandeis University from 1968-70.

BERNARD BARUCH   (1870-1965)   b. Camden, SC

Public Official   The financier turned consultant to virtually every U.S. President of his day served the government during both World Wars as a policy advisor on economic and industrial matters. Regarded as a great elder statesman, he was also a U.S. representative to the UN Atomic Energy Commission (1946), introducing programs to control atomic weapons.

RUDOLPH BOSCHWITZ (1930-) b. Berlin, Germany

U.S. Senator   After earning a law degree, he pursued a successful career in business, entered politics and went on to win elections as Republican senator from Minnesota in 1978 and 1984. He was a staunch supporter of refugee protection and meaningful defense programs. He served with distinction on several committees including Foreign Relations.

BARBARA BOXER (1940-) b. New York City

U.S. Senator   The former Wall Street stockbroker with a degree in economics relocated to California in 1965 and entered local Democratic politics in Marin County. She worked with House Representative John Burton whom she succeeded in 1982. Winning a U.S. Senate seat a decade later, she has since been an outspoken crusader for constituent concerns, with emphasis on women's issues.

DIANNE FEINSTEIN (1933-) b. San Francisco, CA

U.S. Senator   In a political career filled with drama, including filling the unexpired term of an assassinated mayor, she persevered to twice gain the mayoralty on her own and win a full term U.S. Senate seat in 1994. The California Democrat with independent convictions has forcefully supported public land preservation, and assault weapon and drug trafficking control.

ANNA ROSENBERG HOFFMAN (1902-83) b. Budapest, Hungary

Public Official   One of the most influential women in national affairs for a quarter of a century, she served as an assistant secretary of defense (1950-53), the highest ranking woman then in the military. She was also an effective labor relations negotiator and was awarded the Medal of Merit by President Truman, and the Medal of Freedom by President Eisenhower.

131

JACOB JAVITS (1904-86)) b. New York City
U.S. Senator While representing New York State in the U.S. Senate for 24 years, the lawmaker drafted key legislation on foreign affairs, urban redevelopment, civil rights and regulations affecting labor and business. He previously served four terms in the House and as his state's Attorney General. His name is attached to New York City's convention center.

HENRY KISSINGER (1923-) b. Furth, Germany
Secretary of State The eminent statesmen and political theorist advised Presidents John Kennedy, Richard Nixon and Gerald Ford on foreign policy matters. While Nixon's Secretary of State, he was awarded a Nobel Prize for Peace for overseeing the end of the Vietnam War (1973), the same year he also helped arrange a cease-fire in the Arab-Israeli conflict.

IRVING KRISTOL (1920-) b. New York City
Political Scientist The articulate proponent of neo-conservative philosophy was an early advocate of increasing government revenues and investment through tax reductions. The Professor of Social Thought at New York University publishes *The National Interest* and has written for *Commentary*, *The New Leader* and *The Wall Street Journal*.

WILLIAM KRISTOL (1953-)
Political Advisor The outspoken neo-conservative was a top aide to former Vice President Dan Quayle, and was also known for circulating memorandums underpinning a good deal of Republican political strategy. He notes that his purpose is "not to hum quietly, but to change the world." He is the son of the respected conservative writer and commentator, Irving Kristol.

MADELEINE KUNIN (1933-) b. Zurich, Switzerland
State Governor A Harvard University professor and journalist turned politician, she was elected Democratic representative to Vermont's House in 1972, serving three terms. In a narrow 1978 victory, she won the lieutenant governorship to which she was reelected. She filled the governor's seat in 1984, the first woman to hold that office in the State of Vermont.

FIORELLO H. LAGUARDIA (1882-1947) b. New York City
Mayor, New York City The charismatic politician laid the foundations for honest urban government and attracted some of the best people to his immensely popular administration (1934-45). He was among the first to urge federal support for the cities and transformed the infrastructure and look of New York – from the Brooklyn Battery Tunnel to LaGuardia airport.

HERBERT LEHMAN (1878-1963) b. New York City
Governor, New York After a career in banking, he entered public service as New York's lieutenant governor (1928), running on FDR's gubernatorial ticket. His successful bid for state leadership came in 1932, followed by four reelections. During his term, the governor advanced socially progressive legislation for which New York State became a national model.

DAVID E. LILIENTHAL (1899-1981) b. Morton, IL
Chairman, Atomic Energy Commission The specialist in utility law was named vice chairman of the Tennessee Valley Authority, created in 1933 to provide low-cost electric power. Within four years, the T.V.A. became the largest power producer in the Western Hemisphere. He rose to its chairmanship in 1945 and later moved to the helm of America's new Atomic Energy Commission.

GOLDA MEIR   (1898-1978)   b. Kiev, Russia
Israeli Prime Minister She emigrating with her family to Milwaukee at age eight and became a public school teacher active in the Zionist movement in America. Resettling in Palestine in 1921, she was Israel's first ambassador to the USSR (1949), foreign minister (1956-66) and prime minister in 1969. She resigned in 1974, remaining politically involved until her death.

NEWTON MINOW   (1926-)   b. Milwaukee, WI
Public Official The attorney's lengthy political association with Adlai Stevenson was extended to President John F. Kennedy who appointed him head of the FCC in 1961. In that role he expanded the channels and national outreach of TV, while pressing for increased educational programming. In 1964 he authored *Equal time: The Private Broadcasters and the Public Interest.*

HENRY M. MORGENTHAU   (1856-1946)   b. Mannheim, Germany
Financier/Public Official The Columbia University Law School graduate formed several real estate companies in New York City before entering politics and diplomacy. He served as financial chairman of the Democratic National Committee (1912-16) and was appointed ambassador to Turkey by President Woodrow Wilson (1913). He later helped organize the International Red Cross.

HENRY MORGENTHAU, JR.   (1891-1967)   b. New York City
Cabinet Member His financial expertise led President Franklin D. Roosevelt to name him to the Federal Farm Board and later as Treasury Secretary (1934) responsible for funding the New Deal. An ardent supporter of the Allied cause at the start of World War Two, he supervised war bond drives and subsequently helped organize the International Monetary Fund and World Bank.

ROBERT MOSES (1888-1981) b. New Haven, CT
Public Official/Architect With vision and energy, New York State's prolific planner and builder constructed the Triborough and Verrazano-Narrows Bridges, Jones Beach State Park, the St. Lawrence power project and the 1964-65 World's Fair. Once holding twelve public sector posts, he also installed 658 playgrounds, 416 miles of parkway and thirteen other bridges.

MAXWELL RABB (1910-) b. Boston, MA
Public Official After military service the attorney served as a legal consultant to the Secretary of the Navy (1946). Appointed a staff aid to President Eisenhower in 1953, he handled immigration, civil rights and labor issues for the White House. He chaired the U.S. mission at the tenth UNESCO conference (1958) and later joined the NAACP's board of directors.

ABRAHAM RIBICOFF (1910-) b. New Britain, CT
U.S. Senator and Governor Few Americans have matched the public service record of the governor (1955-61) and three-term senator from Connecticut who also sat in the Kennedy cabinet. He was formerly elected as a legislator in the Connecticut General Assembly, and is also remembered for recommending JFK as a vice presidential candidate on the 1956 Democratic ticket.

ISAAC RUBINOW (1875-1936) b. Grodno, Russia
Economist/Social Reformer While serving on a special commission within the American Medical Association in 1916, he became an early advocate for a national health care system. Although he failed in that mission, his reports reached President Franklin D. Roosevelt who retained him as a consultant to the committee that designing the Social Security Act.

135

MARSHALL SHULMAN (1916-) b. Jersey City, NJ
Diplomat/Professor   As one of our nation's leading authorities on U.S.-Soviet relations, he acted as an advisor to the State Department when headed by Dean Acheson and Cyrus Vance. He was director of the Averell Harriman Institute for Advanced Study of the Soviet Union at Columbia University which endowed a professorship in Soviet Foreign Policy in his name (1986).

J. DAVID SINGER (1925-) b. New York City
Political Scientist   His insights on politics, social science, international affairs and defense policy have informed and guided key governmental decision makers. The professor of political science has authored and edited many seminal works in his field, including *Weapons Management in World Politics*, *Explaining War* and *On the Scientific Study of Politics*.

ARLEN SPECTER (1930-) b. Wichita, KS
U.S. Senator   The indomitable Republican campaigner is serving a third senatorial term despite Pennsylvania's strong Democratic tradition. He played active roles in the JFK assassination investigation and the Anita Hill-Clarence Thomas senate committee hearings. The independent-minded legislator occasionally differs in principle with his party's conservative wing.

LEWIS STRAUSS (1896-1974) b. Charleston, WV
Public Official   In 1917, the former shoe salesman assisted Herbert Hoover in our nation's Belgian relief effort, and subsequently gained a partnership in the banking firm of Kuhn Loeb & Company (1919-47). He was appointed rear admiral at the start of World War Two and later served on the U.S. Atomic Energy Commission, eventually as its chairman (1946-58).

ROBERT STRAUSS (1918-) b. Lockhart, TX
Statesman   The authority on Soviet affairs entered national politics in the late 1960s, officiating as Democratic party chairman and President Jimmy Carter's special representative for trade negotiations (1977-79). He later became Carter's personal representative for Middle East negotiations (1979-81) and climaxed his career as U.S. ambassador to the U.S.S.R. in 1991.

BEN WATTENBERG (1933-) b. New York City
Political Advisor/Author   He functioned as counselor to President Lyndon B. Johnson and Senators Hubert Humphrey and Henry Jackson. The co-editor of *Public Opinion Magazine* (1977-89) is associated with the American Enterprise Institute which he co-founded. In addition, he has written many books on domestic politics, the most recent of which is *The Terrain of the Nineties* (1990).

Other Noted People in Government

Abraham Beame
  – second Jewish mayor of New York City

George Beer
  – U.S. delegate to the League of Nations

Sol Bloom
  – helped establish the United Nations organization

Rudy Boschwitz
  – U.S. Senator from the State of Minnesota

Emanuel Celler
  – chairman of the House Judiciary Committee

Abram Elkus
  – ambassador to Turkey during World War One

Hamilton Fish, Jr.
- U.S. Congressman, publisher of *The Nation*

David Garth
- media consultant for ranking political figures

Carl Gershman
- counselor to the U.S. representative to the U.N.

Richard Goodwin
- JFK speech writer and LBJ confidant

Ernest Gruening
- Governor and U.S. Senator from Alaska

Stephen Hess
- staff aide to Presidents Eisenhower and Nixon

Max Kampelman
- headed negotiations for nuclear weapons control

Mickey Kantor
- international trade representative for the U.S.

Theodore Kheel
- mediator of NYC's transit and newspaper strikes

Edward Koch
- blunt, dynamic, four-term NYC mayor, now a columnist

Frank Lautenberg
- U.S. Senator from the State of New Jersey

Carl Levin
- U.S. Senator from the State of Michigan

Frank Licht
- Governor of the State of Rhode Island

Joseph Lieberman
- U.S. Senator from the State of Connecticut

Julius Meier
- Governor of the State of Oregon

Howard Metzenbaum
 – U.S. Senator from the State of Ohio

Bess Myerson
 – former Miss America, NYC consumer affairs chief

Maud Nathan
 – influential early campaigner for women's suffrage

David Niles
 – aide and advisor to Presidents FDR and Truman

Richard Pipes
 – sovietologist on the National Security Council

Isador Rayner
 – U.S. Congressman and Senator from Maryland

Felix Rohatyn
 – headed Municipal Assistance Corp. of NYC

Eugene Rostow
 – enacted President Reagan's arms control policies

Walt Rostow
 – national security affairs advisor to LBJ

Arthur Seligman
 – Governor of the State of New Mexico

Milton Shapp
 – Governor of the State of Pennsylvania

Laurence Steinhardt
 – ambassador to Peru, the USSR and Canada

Oscar Straus
 – appointed by four presidents to high office

Adam Yarmolinsky
 – helped guide domestic policy for JFK and LBJ

James Zellerbach
 – U.S. ambassador to Italy

People in the Law

ALBERT BLAUSTEIN (1921-1994) b. New York City
Legal Scholar The attorney occupied his career drafting constitutions that established the legal, moral and political character of
foreign governments. Since 1966 he tailored constitutions for
Liberia and Fiji, and contributed to those of Zimbabwe, Bangla-
desh, Peru, Nicaragua, Romania and post-Soviet Russia – among
the forty nations for which he helped design such documents.

LOUIS BRANDEIS (1856-1941) b. Louisville, KY
U.S. Supreme Court Justice A foremost legal mind of his day, he
was best known for rulings that protected the rights of individuals
against powerful commercial and business interests. His career as
a liberal attorney and judge peaked with his 1916 appointment to
the high court by President Woodrow Wilson. He was among the
leading supporters of New Deal legislation on that court.

BENJAMIN CARDOZO (1870-1938) b. New York City
U.S. Supreme Court Justice Although a liberal, he won conservative President Herbert Hoover's respect for his judicial integrity
and legal knowledge and was named by Hoover to the Supreme
Court (1932). He previously served on the New York Supreme
Court and was noted for the literary quality of his written opinions,
many of which involved laws enacted during FDR's New Deal.

ALAN DERSHOWITZ (1938-) b. New York City
Trial Lawyer As much a celebrity as those he often represents, he
is a crusader for justice often retained by controversial clients.
High-profile defenses were typically mounted for hotel magnate
Leona Helmsley, socialite Claus von Bulow and evangelist Jim
Bakker. He was Harvard's youngest law professor, has authored
legal texts and writes a syndicated column.

ABRAHAM FORTAS (1910-82) b. Memphis, TN
U.S. Supreme Court Justice He entered government as counsel for the Public Works Administration (1937) and was an advisor to the conference establishing the U.N. where he befriended Lyndon B. Johnson. Upon assuming the presidency, LBJ appointed him personal advisor and later named him to the Supreme Court. His term lasted from 1968 until he resigned the following year.

FELIX FRANKFURTER (1882-1965) b. Vienna, Austria
U.S. Supreme Court Justice His intellect and judicial sensibility made his tenure as Supreme Court Justice (1939-62) productive and historic. To this day, his opinions are often quoted as legal precedents. He was a founder of the Civil Liberties Union, and helped formulate progressive labor laws and defended the powers assumed by local governments and lower courts.

RUTH BADER GINSBURG (1933-) b. New York City
U.S. Supreme Court Justice She was appointed the first female full professor at Columbia Law School in 1972, and became the second woman to serve on the high court in 1993. A constitutionalist committed to equal protection under the law, she has vigorously supported measures to remove barriers to opportunity restricting both genders.

ARTHUR J. GOLDBERG (1908-90) b. Chicago, IL
U.S. Supreme Court Justice The graduate of Northwestern University Law School (1929) achieved a reputation as a labor lawyer during FDR's administration, and set up anti-fascist clandestine operations during World War Two. He later served as Secretary of Labor under President John F. Kennedy (1960-2), as a high court justice (1962-5) and as United Nations ambassador (1965-8).

ARTHUR GARFIELD HAYS (1881-1954) b. Rochester, NY
Civil Liberties Attorney He was associated with some of the century's most sensational legal cases, earlier as co-counsel with Clarence Darrow at the Scopes' "monkey" trial in 1925. Others included the Sacco-Vanzetti "anarchist" trial (1927) and his defense of Communists falsely accused of setting fire to the Reichstag, Germany's parliament building.

LOUIS NIZER (1902-94) b. London, England
Trial Lawyer For more than six decades, he was a flamboyant figure in courtrooms, representing celebrities including Mae West, Charley Chaplin and Johnny Carson. His mastery of contract and libel law drew many clients from the entertainment industry. A prolific author, he also gained attention for his graphic bestselling autobiography *My Life in Court* (1962).

Other Noted People in the Law

Benjamin Cohen
– drafted much of FDR's New Deal legislation

Richard Epstein
– legal theoretician at University of Chicago

Jerome Frank
– helped administer the New Deal during the 1930s

Leonard Garment
– Watergate defense counsel to President Nixon

Rita Hauser
– former U.S. representative to the United Nations

William Kunstler
– activist defender of civil rights cases

142

Nathan Lewin
– highly respected constitutional lawyer and scholar

Louis Marshall
– pioneering, outspoken civil rights advocate

Adam Mikva
– counselor to leaders in all branches of government

Joseph Rauh
– noted defender of human rights and civil liberties

Samuel Rosenman
– counselor to Presidents Roosevelt and Truman

Jerome Shestak
– co-founder of the Legal Services Corporation

Simon Wiesenthal
– exposes Nazi war criminals worldwide

People in the Military

CLAUDE BLOCH (1878-1967) b. Woodbury, KY
Admiral His rise from decorated officer in the Spanish-American war to commander-in-chief of the U.S. Fleet (1938-40) spanned many naval actions in which he took part. He saw combat duty in 1900 during China's Boxer rebellion, served as a naval transport commander during World War One, and later captained the battleship *California* with the rank of rear admiral. He retired in 1942.

JUDITH RESNICK (1949-86) b. Cleveland, OH
Astronaut The explosion of the shuttle Challenger in 1986 ended the life of the first Jewish astronaut to enter space. A classical pianist, as well as a biomedical and systems engineer with a Ph.D., she had earlier logged 145 hours as a mission specialist aboard Discovery. Adventures in space were dreams of a woman with a lifelong ambition "...to do everything there is to be done."

HYMAN RICKOVER (1900-86) b. Makow, Russia

Admiral The outspoken naval crusader was the father of America's nuclear powered submarine force which assured our dominance under the seas. He had introduced infrared signalling and magnetic mine sweepers into naval warfare. He also headed the joint Navy-Atomic Energy Commission, was promoted to admiral in 1973 and twice received Congressional Gold Medals.

Other Noted People in the Military

August Bondi
– fought with John Brown against pro-slavery forces

Edward Ellsberg
– rear admiral, authority on raising sunken ships

Adolph Marix
– first Jewish rear admiral, commander of the *Maine*

Eight
Science, Medicine and Invention

One million homes and businesses in the U.S. were equipped with telephones at the turn of the century. Electric lights, motor cars and other technological and scientific marvels born of American ingenuity had begun transforming our world. During this era of leapfrogging change, many Jews brought ideas and energy to science, medicine and invention.

While the following statistics were gathered about a decade ago, they have not since changed drastically, and from then to now, the percentage of Jews in the U.S. population stands at a steady two to three percent.

In 1983, Jewish-American scientists received 27% of the Nobel Prizes awarded in their disciplines. In proportion to the nation's population, the number of Jews in medicine exceeded 230%, those is psychiatry neared 480% and those in mathematics approached 240%. There are reasons for records such as these.

A characteristic attitude and behavior prepared Jews for life in separate spiritual and physical worlds. Seldom denying their Jewishness, they freely ventured into secular society. Immigrant parents for the most part encouraged and supported their children's "Americanization." Education was a catalyst, and members of the younger generation today are twice as likely to attend college than are non-Jewish students. And they are apt to excel in the sciences and health professions.

What motivates Jews to study and learn is the common belief that education is, above all, a pathway to success and status. "You shall teach your children" is a tenet from the bible heeded by Jewish parents for thousands of years.

In the new land, increased educational opportunity, coupled with benign social and legal conditions, served the children of the immigrants well. What better atmosphere for attracting and nurturing free-thinking scientists?

Casting off the baggage of repressive European societies, Jewish scientists also fled to our shores in large numbers before World War Two and, by their example, fostered a love for their disciplines in generations to come. They stood in the shadow of such monuments to the healing arts as Sigmund Freud who invented psychiatry and August von Wassermann whose diagnostic test would help contain the then rampant disease of syphilis.

From Albert Einstein to Isidor Rabi to Rosalyn Yalow – Nobel Laureates all – comes a heritage of intellect, imagination and curiosity shared by Jewish peers in the classrooms, laboratories and medical centers of our nation.

Scientists

FRANZ BOAS (1858-1942) b. Minden, Germany
Anthropologist His use of statistical analysis and scientific methodology in studying language, race and culture built the foundations of American anthropology. The Columbia University professor travelled widely to Eskimo and Indian homelands to confirm theories he presented in such classics as *The Mind of Primitive Man* (1938) and *Race, Language and Culture* (1940).

RICHARD COURANT (1888-1972) b. Lublinitz, Germany
Mathematician The director of New York University's Courant Research Institute (1953-8) applied principles of quantum mechanics to solving complex problems in physics. His advanced methods contributed toward early developments in computer design. The escapee from Nazi oppression also supervised scientific programs for the U.S. military during World War Two.

ALBERT EINSTEIN (1879-1955) b. Ulm, Germany
Physicist Among the achievements of the century's greatest theoretical physicist were his Nobel Prize-winning application of quantum mechanics to photoelectricity (1921), an analysis of Brownian motion, and several theories of relativity which revolutionized our concepts of time and space. His famous equation, $E=MC^2$, helped enable the atomic age.

BERNARD FELD (1919-93) b. New York City
Physicist The colleague of physicist Enrico Fermi was a member of the team that developed the atom bomb. Leaving government research programs in 1945, he spent his remaining years pressing for an end to the arms race. He founded the Federation of American Scientists to support his mission and later assumed the presidency of the Albert Einstein Peace Foundation.

JEROME FRIEDMAN (1930-) b. Chicago, IL
Physicist The co-recipient of a Nobel Prize for Physics in 1990 conducted experiments on a linear accelerator and demonstrated that neutrons and protons were formed of quarks, the fundamental energy packets from which all matter is composed. A professor at the Massachusetts Institute of Technology since 1960, he headed the school's physics department from 1983 to 1988.

MURRAY GELL-MANN (1929-) b. New York City
Physicist He studied and clarified the puzzling phenomenon of elementary subatomic particles, classifying them as "quarks" within an ordering system he called the Eightfold Way. The achievement earned him the Nobel Prize for Physics in 1969. He also served on the faculties of Chicago University, Princeton University and the California Institute of Technology.

DONALD GLASER (1926-) b. Cleveland, OH
Physicist Mapping the movements of high-speed atomic particles was imprecise until he developed an innovative approach to nuclear tracking. By modifying the way in which conventional cloud chambers trace the paths of particles, he invented the bubble chamber which is today the basic tool for plotting subatomic motion. His work won a 1960 Nobel Prize for Physics.

ROBERT HOFSTADTER (1915-90) b. New York City
Physicist With findings drawn from his research on a particle accelerator, he shed light on atomic structure and helped create an identifying order for subatomic particles. He also correctly predicted the existence of the omega-meson and rho-meson. These feats, coupled with his studies of controlled nuclear fission, earned a Nobel Prize for Physics in 1961.

ALBERT MICHELSON (1852-1931) b. Strelno, Prussia
Physicist The results of his experiment that accurately determined the speed of light underpinned Albert Einstein's theory of relativity. Regarded as a key finding in scientific history, the discovery was made on an instrument he invented and is used today to measure the wavelengths of spectrums. He was the first American to win a Nobel Prize for Physics (1907).

J. ROBERT OPPENHEIMER (1904-67) b. New York City
Physicist His leadership of the Manhattan Project laboratory during World War Two earned him the title, "Father of the Atomic Bomb." Subsequently, he became director of the Institute for Advanced Study in Princeton (1947-66) and chaired the general advisory committee of the U.S. Atomic Energy Commission. He was an eloquent advocate of civilian control over atomic energy.

ARNO PENZIAS (1933-) b. Munich, Germany
Physicist While conducting research on microwave transmission at Bell Laboratories, he stumbled on a phenomenon tracing back to the origin of the universe – highly diffuse cosmic radiation left over after the Big Bang. His discovery earned a 1978 Nobel Prize for Physics. The radio astronomer and astrophysicist also holds two patents in the field of communications technology.

ISIDOR RABI (1898-1988) b. Rymanow, Austro-Hungary
Physicist His many appointments included positions at Columbia University and the Massachusetts Institute of Technology, Brookhaven National Laboratory for Atomic Research, and the U.N. Science Committee. He was best known for breakthrough research on molecular beams, magnetism and quantum mechanics, and was awarded a Nobel Prize for Physics in 1944.

CARL SAGAN (1934-) b. New York City
Astrophysicist The world's preeminent and most visible popularizer of astronomy, space flight and cosmology has written more than twenty books including the bestsellers *Broca's Brain* (1979), *Contact* (1985) and *The Dragons of Eden* (Pulitzer Prize 1977). His award-winning production *Cosmos* was televised in sixty countries to more than a half billion viewers.

HERBERT SIMON (1916-) b. Milwaukee, WI
Computer Scientist This visionary in the world of computers and artificial intelligence received a Nobel Prize for Economics (1978) and National Medal of Science (1986). Among his creations were problem-solving software programs and computer languages. He also pursues the design of information systems that would accurately project economic models of the world's nations.

149

EDWARD TELLER (1908-) b. Budapest, Hungary
Physicist While involved in A-bomb research at the Manhattan Project, he pressed for co-development of a far more powerful weapon: the H-bomb. Its successful test explosion in 1952 reinforced our nation's superpower status. He also headed the radiation laboratory at Livermore, CA, and was a professor of physics at the University of California, Berkeley (1953-75).

Other Noted Scientists

Bernard Cohen
– developed procedures to measure radon levels

Kasimir Fajans
– formulated the theory of how isotopes react

Enrico Fermi
– world-renowned atomic physicist and theoretician

Oscar Julius
– former president of the American Chemical Society

Jacob Lipman
– soil chemist, a scientific farming pioneer

Joseph Rosen
– agronomist, discovered prime strains of winter rye

Frank Schlessinger
– astronomer, director of Yale Observatory

Leo Szilard
– co-developer of atomic chain reaction system

Norbert Weiner
– conceived and evolved the science of cybernetics

Health Professionals

ALFRED ADLER (1870-1937) b. Vienna, Austria
Psychiatrist The associate of Sigmund Freud (1902-11) severed their relationship when disagreeing with a central Freudian thesis. He held that emotional states were primarily controlled by ambitions in conflict with an inferiority complex, rather than by sex. He strongly influenced American and European psychiatry and authored a seminal work *The Neurotic Constitution* in 1912.

SIDNEY ALTMAN (1939-) b. Montreal, Canada
Molecular Biologist He shared a 1989 Nobel Prize for Chemistry with Thomas Cech for simultaneously discovering that RNA molecules could reorganize themselves without enzymes, and directly affect chemical reactions within cells. His work advanced knowledge of how genetic data is transferred, and how the body's defenses can be strengthened against viral attack.

BRUNO BETTELHEIM (1903-90) b. Vienna, Austria
Psychoanalyst A survivor of Nazi concentration camps, he pioneered psychoanalytic procedures for helping treat emotionally disturbed children. He also studied the formative effects of parenting or caregiving on child behavior. Among his best known books for general audiences were *Love Is Not Enough* (1950), *The Uses of Enchantment* (1976) and *Freud and Man's Soul* (1983).

GERTRUDE ELION (1918-) b. New York City
Biochemist The co-recipient of the Nobel Prize for Physiology or Medicine (1989) designed studies that led to formulating many new drugs now used to inhibit the progress of leukemia. Her work also shed light on how DNA functions. She was also the first woman elected to the National Inventors Hall of Fame (1991) which honors figures such as Thomas Alva Edison.

151

MORRIS FISHBEIN (1889-1976) b. St. Louis, MO
Physician The editor of the prestigious *Journal of the American Medical Association* (1924-49) was an authoritative and formidable spokesperson for the policies and practices of American medicine. He wrote copiously and lectured on medical and public health issues, strongly condemning medical quackery. His health column appeared in a number of leading U.S. dailies.

ERICH FROMM (1900-80) b. Frankfort, Germany
Psychoanalyst He was a neo-Freudian applying classic psychoanalytic theories to the study of cultures and people. He felt that wholesome human relationships, a productive lifestyle and unselfish love buoy up emotional health in modern, impersonal industrial societies. Among his most significant books were *Escape from Freedom* (1941) and *The Art of Loving* (1956).

CASIMIR FUNK (1884-1967) b. Warsaw, Poland
Biochemist While studying the deficiency disease, beriberi, in England's Lister Institute, he found a preventive which he named a "vitamine." He also discovered the efficacy of sex hormones in treating various illnesses. The scientist became a consultant for the U.S. Vitamin Corporation in 1936, and later founded and headed the Funk Foundation for Medical Research.

WALTER GILBERT (1932-) b. Cambridge, MA
Biologist A Harvard professor since 1959, he was co-recipient of the Nobel Prize for Chemistry (1980) for breakthroughs in molecular biology that advanced the science of genetic engineering. He formed several companies to capitalize on his discoveries: Biogen Inc. (1978), a biotechnology firm, and Genome Corp. (1987), which is currently mapping the human genetic blueprint.

JOSEPH GOLDBERGER (1874-1929) b. Giralt, Hungary
Pathologist Pellagra was a debilitating illness largely affecting Americans in the southeast. While a career employee with the U.S. Public Health Service he identified the condition as a nutritional deficiency which could be prevented or cured by Vitamin B_2, which he isolated. He also helped introduce new methods for managing infectious ailments.

MATHILDE KRIM (1926-) b. Como, Italy
Geneticist/Virologist In addition to conducting advanced research into the causes and treatment of cancer and AIDS, she is a tireless health educator. Her fund-raising campaigns financed a molecular-virology laboratory for AIDS research at St. Luke's-Roosevelt Hospital Center in New York. She is also associated with Columbia University's College of Physicians and Surgeons.

JOSHUA LEDERBERG (1925-) b. Montclair, NJ
Geneticist He shared the 1958 Nobel Prize for Physiology or Medicine with Edward Tatum for landmark work in microbial genetics. His co-discovery that bacteria exchange genetic materials established for the first time that such microorganisms can reproduce sexually. He became director of the Kennedy Laboratories for Molecular Biology and Medicine in 1961.

PHILIP LEVINE (1900-87) b. Kletsk, Russia
Immunologist While studying blood antibodies and serums, he discovered and co-discovered several key constituents, including the Rh factor, which significantly safeguard blood transfusions and protect newborns. His research, which received many honors, was conducted at New York's Rockefeller Institute, New Jersey's Beth Israel Hospital and the Ortho Research Foundation.

153

OTTO LOEWI (1873-1961) b. Frankfort, Germany
Pharmacologist He investigated how vital organs respond to chemical and electrical stimulation, and established their dependence on certain proteins for proper function. As a result, he learned how nerve impulses are transmitted by chemical messengers. His findings helped advance medical therapy and earned him the 1936 Nobel Prize for Physiology or Medicine.

IRWIN MANDEL (1922-) b. New York City
Dental Scientist The ADA Gold Medal Award for Excellence in Dental Research he received in 1985 is dentistry's counterpart of the Nobel Prize. His studies broadened understanding of dental disease and of saliva as a diagnostic tool. In recognition of his worldwide contributions to oral health, he was also awarded a prestigious honorary doctorate from Sweden's University of Goteborg (1984).

OTTO RANK (1884-1939) b. Vienna, Austria
Psychoanalyst The disciple of Sigmund Freud left his mentor in 1925 to independently develop a theory that viewed birth trauma as a primary cause of emotional stress and anxiety. Before emigrating to the U.S. in 1935, he wrote an acknowledged masterpiece on incest myths. His later works sifted through mythology and the arts for useful psychoanalytic insights.

THEODOR REIK (1888-1968) b. Vienna, Austria
Psychoanalyst In opposition to Sigmund Freud, he insisted that the death wish of masochists is their misdirected way of seeking happiness. Another theory he originated maintained that crime is driven by unconscious guilt and a demand for punishment. His fifty books, many for lay readers, broadened and enriched current knowledge of human motivation and behavior.

ALBERT SABIN (1906-) b. Bialystok, Poland
Physician/Microbiologist His medical research led to a live, orally administered vaccine (1959) which became the treatment of choice for polio prevention worldwide. He also investigated viral causes of infectious diseases and a possible virus-cancer link. He was elected to the American Academy of Arts and Sciences, and to the National Academy of Sciences.

JONAS E. SALK (1914-95) b. New York City
Biologist He discovered an anti-polio vaccine which was licensed for use in 1955. Since its introduction, his and Albert Sabin's immunizing agents have virtually driven the paralyzing disease from the U.S. and most of the world. His search for advanced vaccines continued at the University of California's Institute for Biological Research which he directed until his death.

GEORGE WALD (1906-) b. New York City
Biologist While researching the biochemistry of vision at Harvard University, he disclosed the presence of Vitamin A in the retina of the eye. Further discoveries of the molecular makeup and chemical interactions within the eyes of all species won him the Nobel Prize for Physiology or Medicine in 1967. He was also politically engaged on behalf of international peace movements.

LILLIAN WALD (1867-1940) b. Cincinnati, OH
Social Worker The most effective social worker and public health advocate of her time established a visiting nurse service in New York and a medical treatment program for school children. Her activism helped the U.S. achieve world leadership in fielding such services. Another monument to her work was the Henry Street Settlement which she founded in 1893 and headed for forty years.

DAVID WECHSLER (1896-1981) b. Lespedi, Romania
Psychologist Standardized forms of his intelligence tests have been universally used for measuring reasoning ability and mental acuity with great sensitivity and accuracy. His tests contain procedures for tracking intellectual performance by age and for diagnosing brain abnormalities. He was chief psychologist at New York's Bellevue Psychiatric Hospital from 1932 to 1966.

ROSALYN YALOW (1921-) b. New York City
Medical Researcher The first American woman to receive the Nobel Prize in her discipline (1977) was honored for a major contribution to medicine and physiology. She developed the radioimmunoassay, a complex analytical procedure that measures the amount of biological substances in the blood. The process opened doors to many lifesaving discoveries.

Other Noted Health Professionals

David Baltimore
– Nobelist enlisted in the battle against AIDS

Abraham Brill
– translator of Sigmund Freud's work into English

Edwin Cohen
– his innovations modernized blood plasma usage

Leo Davidoff
– a foremost American neuro-surgeon

Carl Djerassi
– synthesized the world's first oral contraceptive

Isaac Djerassi
– physician and noted cancer researcher

156

Gerald Edelman
– Nobelist now studying brain and mind linkage

Paul Ehrlich
– biologist and crusader for population control

Max Einhorn
– invented instruments to diagnose intestinal ills

Charles Elsberg
– known for advances in brain and heart surgery

Simon Flexner
– isolated type-B dysentery bacillus

Judah Folkman
– spearheaded research in the fight against cancer

Willard Gaylin
– psychoanalyst and expert on bioethics

Richard Goldschmidt
– propounded key theory of genetic mutation

Kurt Goldstein
– psychiatrist, author of *The Nature of Man*

Howard Hiatt
– dean of Harvard School of Public Health

Abraham Jacobi
– pediatrician who invented the laryngoscope

Joseph Jastrow
– author of numerous popular books on psychology

Nathan Kline
– psychiatrist, introduced modern tranquilizers

Henry Koplik
– founder of the American Pediatric Society

Jacques Loeb
– biologist who advanced the theory of "tropisms"

157

Frederick Perls
- psychiatrist, formulator of Gestalt therapy

Gregory Pincus
- developed first practical birth control pill

Milton J. Rosenau
- founder of Harvard's School of Public Health

Oliver Sacks
- neurologist and author of *Awakenings*

Joshua Sakel
- pioneered insulin shock to treat mental disorder

Bela Schick
- his test predicts susceptibility to diphtheria

Arthur Shapiro
- advanced the treatment of Tourette's Syndrome

Howard Tager
- increased understanding of diabetes and insulin

Selman Waksman
- discovered the wonder drug streptomycin

Inventors

CHARLES ADLER JR. (1899-1990) b. Baltimore, MD
Inventor More than sixty patents cover the safety devices he independently invented. Among them were traffic signals activated by sound and by approaching cars, stop lights for the color blind, and double-filament lamps used in railroad signals. He was cited for patriotism at donating the patent for an electronic collision warning device to the government in 1956.

EMILE BERLINER (1851-1929) b. Hanover, Germany
Inventor/Industrialist He developed a practical alternative to Thomas Edison's phonograph in 1887: the Victor Talking Ma-

chine which replaced the cylinder with a disk and sired a vast industry. Years earlier, his microphone-receiver had made the Bell telephone a workable reality. He also spoke out for pasteurization and sponsored royalty rights for performing artists.

HAROLD P. BROWN (1908-) b. Grandby, MO
Research Chemist He specialized in the development of adhesives, sealants and coatings and earned thirty patents in his field. His formulation of a family of polymers that swelled when immersed in water found widespread commercial applications. He was long associated with chemistry departments of leading universities and the research laboratories of B.F. Goodrich.

LEOPOLD GODOWSKY JR. (1901-83) b. Chicago, IL
Inventor In collaboration with Leopold Mannes during the 1920s, he created a practical color film process he brought to Kodak when joining the photography giant's R&D staff. The final development of Kodachrome film came in 1936. His team helped devise other types of Kodak color film over the years. He was married to the sister of George and Ira Gershwin.

EDWIN LAND (1909-91) b. Norwich, CT
Inventor As legend has it, his young daughter asked why photos did not appear after clicking the camera, upon which the self-taught physicist began his research. The world was introduced to instant photography in 1948 by his Polaroid Land Camera, and a 1960s survey found half of the nation's households possessing one or more. He retired in 1982 with 544 patents to his name.

SAMUEL RUBEN (1900-88) b. New York City
Inventor The long-lived alkaline battery is but one of more than 300 patented inventions from the mind of a research scientist with

no formal education beyond high school. His dry electrolytic condensers are in the systems of most electric motor starters, and were standard components for decades in almost every television and radio set manufactured.

CHARLES P. STEINMETZ (1865-1923) b: Breslau, Germany
Electrical Engineer   General Electric Company's chief consulting engineer was granted hundreds of design patents for advanced electric motors and dynamos. His fame also rested on electrical devices for conducting high voltage power over long distances and for the "law of hysteresis," a formula applied to increasing the operating efficiency of electrical equipment.

Other Noted Inventors

Elias Riess
  – his converter electrified the nation's railroads

Arthur Korn
  – pioneered transmitting photos via electrical wire

Carl Neuberg
  – created a process to convert sugar into glycerine

Nine
Business, Industry and Labor

A flood of immigrants poured into New York, Philadelphia and Baltimore at the turn of the century, and a pattern was set. Some turned New York City's Lower East Side into a vast clothing factory and shopping district. Others built thriving businesses in remote towns and cities.

What drove many was the entrepreneurial spirit, and, frequently, the commercial skills they gained as itinerant peddlers and small goods merchants in Europe. A number of newcomers formed import-export enterprises through overseas connections with distant families and friends. Some established close-knit businesses bridging the old and new worlds, as did the Rothschilds in Europe.

The melting pot was stirred by the conviction that success in America demanded self-reliance and respect for the work ethic. More pointedly than other ethnic groups, Jews knew from their long history of exclusion that success was self-made, not given.

America was seen as a clean slate on which ambitious citizens could write their rags-to-riches stories. Freedom of opportunity and education made it so. As a group, Jews have prevailed in corporate leadership, merchandising, marketing, advertising, public relations, economics, banking and real estate. Labor unions formed by Samuel Gompers and David Dubinsky improved the lot of working families aspiring to passage into middle class America.

Examples are many and a few are outstanding. Joseph Hirshhorn, a billionaire born to tenement poverty, owned 600 uranium mines, outnumbering all such operations in the nation. Norton Simon climbed from modest means to launch a food products company ranked with the nation's top hundred. The fabled George Soros is a financial wizard whose corporate assets exceed $11 billion.

Others include multi-billionaire Walter Annenberg, a former U.S. ambassador at the helm of a vast publishing empire. Jack Dreyfus spurred economic breakthroughs for small investors by popularizing mutual funds through his Dreyfus fund. And Simon Guggenheim amassed a fortune from metal smelting and refining.

As philanthropists, and like many successful Jewish business people, they have also given generously to worthy causes in gratitude to the country that enabled their wealth. Hirshhorn and Simon created two notable American museums. Annenberg and Dreyfus separately founded a prominent research institute and a medical foundation. And the Guggenheim name is attached to a foundation assisting scholars, writers and artists, and to a renowned New York City museum of art.

They were not alone in contributing jointly to the prosperity of America and to the welfare of its people. Some of those who followed in their footsteps appear below.

Business, Corporate and Industrial Leaders

BENJAMIN ALTMAN (1840-1913) b. New York City
Merchant/Philanthropist The former owner of a modest dry-goods store transformed New York's suburban shopping scene when forming B. Altman & Company in 1906. His fashionable department stores catered to upscale patrons, setting the tone for competing chains. He deeded his $20 million art collection to the Metropolitan Museum and created a $30 million charitable foundation.

LOUIS BAMBERGER (1855-1944) b. Baltimore, MD
Merchant/Philanthropist His lifetime association with New Jersey brought the state the highly successful L. Bamberger and Company department store and Newark radio station WOR. The enlightened labor policies he practiced became national models. In addition to unsparing support to the Newark Museum, he contributed millions to Princeton's Institute for Advanced Study.

ISAAC BERNHEIM (1848-1945) b. Schmieheim, Germany
Industrialist/Philanthropist He was co-owner of a distillery ranked with the most prominent of the period, and a generous contributor to his adopted city's institutions and public welfare programs. His beneficence brought the first YMHA to the citizens of Louisville, KY, as well as munificent support for the community's hospital and educational systems.

JOSEPH L. BLOCK (1902-92) b. Chicago, IL
Corporate Executive As highly regarded for his civic activities as for his business judgement, he advanced rapidly from the marketing and finance departments of Inland Steel Company to its chairmanship in 1959. He also served with the War Production Board in 1944 and on President's Advisory Committees during the Kennedy, Johnson and Nixon administrations.

ALFRED BLOOMINGDALE (1916-82) b. New York City
Credit Card Pioneer A vision of plastic replacing paper money inspired his drive to universalize consumer credit cards. He reached that goal as president of the Diners' Club whose credit card concept was adopted by the world. The grandson of Bloomingdale Department Store's founder also served on President Ronald Reagan's Foreign Intelligence Advisory Board in 1981.

SAMUEL BLOOMINGDALE (1873-1968) b. New York City
Merchant/Philanthropist The trained architect inherited control of his family's department store in 1905 and increased its fortunes through creative retailing and expansion. He served as its president for a quarter century. Bloomingdale Brothers was founded in 1886 by a relative and Civil War veteran, Lyman Gustavus, a philanthropist-supporter of the Metropolitan Museum of Art..

SIMON BRENTANO (1859-1915) b. Cincinnati, OH
Bookseller   Under his leadership, the enterprise founded in 1858 by his uncle August became one of the world's largest within several decades. During the late Eighties, he began an expansion which built a national bookstore chain. While president, he also authored a book on fire control techniques which was read internationally by public safety professionals.

PETER DRUCKER (1909-) b. Vienna, Austria
Business Consultant   He proposed systems for analyzing and restructuring modern corporations for greater efficiency – a practice now utilized in many organizations and institutions. Among his most widely accepted ideas is "Management by Objectives," and others of equal effectiveness in his award-winning writings about business and corporate culture.

ARMAND FEIGENBAUM (1920-) b. New York City
Quality Control Expert   "Quality is what the customer says it is," is the motto of an international guru of quality control who brought his concepts to Japan during the 1950s. His ideas on management for quality assurance and employee satisfaction have since been adopted by major U.S. companies, spurring their global competitiveness and saving them billions of dollars.

EDWARD FILENE (1860-1937) b. Salem, MA
Merchant/Merchandising Innovator   After taking control of his father's Boston-based department store (1908), he and his brother Albert reinvented retail merchandising through bargain basement sales, and gave fringe and wage incentives never before offered to employees. He was a founder of the U.S. Chamber of Commerce and chief developer of consumer cooperatives and credit unions.

RAYMOND FIRESTONE (1908-94) b. Akron, OH
Industrialist/Philanthropist   The ex-World War Two pilot and auto tire magnate served in many capacities in his family business before gaining its chairmanship (1966-76). Under his leadership, annual sales of the Firestone Tire and Rubber Company rose from $1.4 to $3.9 billion. He gave generously to charitable and educational organizations, including Princeton University.

AVERY FISHER (1906-) b. New York City
Business Leader/Philanthropist   Fisher Radio, founded in 1937, was among the most trusted and prominent designers and manufacturers of advanced stereo units for hi-fi enthusiasts. Upon the sales success of his systems, he endowed the New York Philharmonic with $10 million to completely refurbish its concert hall which bears his name in commemoration.

BRUCE GIMBEL (1913-80) b. New York City
Merchant/Philanthropist   The scion of Adam Gimbel, founder of the department store chain in 1842, followed his father Bernard in the family's great merchandising tradition. He became CEO and chairman in 1973. The decorated World War Two Air Transport Command pilot actively participated in aviation throughout his life. He was also a major patron of Yale University.

MEYER GUGGENHEIM (1828-1905) b. Lengnau, Switzerland
Industrialist/Philanthropist   Mining and refining metals earned a fortune for the father and seven sons of the merchant family. Almost all have given sizeable portions of their personal wealth to public foundations and worthy causes. The most visible civic gesture was made by son Solomon (1861-1939): the Guggenheim Museum in New York City, a pantheon of abstract art.

ARMAND HAMMER (1898-1990) b. New York City
Industrialist   The licensed but non-practicing M.D. devoted his early career to trade-making with the USSR, partly to promote mutual harmony and prosperity. By midlife he built a fortune buying and selling distilleries. During his last decades he shepherded the failing Occidental Petroleum Corporation into the nation's sixteenth largest industrial concern.

JOSEPH HIRSHHORN (1899-1981) b. Mitvau, Latvia
Industrialist/Philanthropist   The fortune he amassed as a stockbroker before the 1929 crash financed Canadian gold and uranium mines which compounded his wealth. A large portion of it purchased a sizeable collection of contemporary art and sculpture which he bequeathed to the American people. The Washington D.C. museum that bears his name houses nearly 6,000 of his artworks.

DONNA KARAN (1948-) b. Forest Hills, NY
Fashion Designer\Businesswoman   Since the premiere of her fashion line in 1985, she has catapulted to the top ranks of clothing designers for women. Her versatile and sophisticated apparel aims to suit executive working women and frequent travelers without sacrificing femininity or flair. Her label has found favor among active women with little time to shop.

ESTEE LAUDER (1910-) b. New York City
Cosmetologist/Businesswoman   A prominent name in beauty culture, she placed glamour within easy reach of women through an all-inclusive line of cosmetics launched in the 1930s. Her marketing techniques, demonstrations and giveaway sample programs helped build a global organization. Many of her formulations have set industrywide standards for quality and value.

RALPH LAUREN   (1939-)   b. New York City
Fashion Designer/Businessman   The president of an exception-
ally successful designer clothing enterprise introduced a look of
casual elegance in lines of men's and women's wear. Many styles
have won Coty Awards for fashion. In a nod to his talent, he was
selected to create Robert Redford's wardrobe in *The Great Gatsby*,
a period drama in which style and fashion played a colorful role.

SAMUEL LEFRAK   (1918-)   b. New York City
Builder/Developer/Philanthropist   He left his mark on the Jersey City waterfront with immense residential and commercial
developments, and in Lower Manhattan with Battery Park City's
high-rise complex. His company also produces middle-income
housing and is among the largest landlords in New York City. He
pursued a parallel career of philanthropic giving to civic institutions.

ABRAHAM LEVITT   (1880-1962)   b. New York City
Builder/Philanthropist   The Levittown communities his firm developed in New York, New Jersey and Pennsylvania were national
models of affordable, mass-prefabricated residences. He helped
revolutionize post-World War Two housing, built more than
140,000 homes and established the Levitt Foundation in 1949 to
support scholarship, medical and welfare programs.

ADOLPH LEWISOHN   (1849-1938)   b. Hamburg, Germany
Industrialist/Philanthropist   The profitable business he established with brothers Leonard and Julius (1867) mined and exported
copper and lead internationally. He also gave generously to his
community, promoting child welfare and prison reform, and supporting New York's colleges and museums. His most visible gift
was an outdoor musical stadium in his name.

167

SOL LINOWITZ (1913-) b. Trenton, NJ
Business Leader/Public Official The World War Two veteran was elected to head Xerox International, Inc. in 1959, and oversaw its rapid growth. Entering public service, he worked with the U.S. State Department and federal poverty programs. He was also appointed U.S. ambassador to the Organization of American States (1966-69) during President Lyndon B. Johnson's administration.

LUCIUS LITTAUER (1859-1944) b. Gloversville, NY
Industrialist/Congressman/Philanthropist The U.S. Congressman from New York (1897-1907) donated profits from his family's huge glove factory and other businesses to educational and medical programs. Included were grants to needy students, a building for the National Hospital for Speech Disorders and a new graduate school for Harvard University.

MICHAEL MILKEN
Investment Banker Recent legal problems have not discredited his creative remaking of corporate America with high yield securities (junk bonds) issued in the 1980s, producing hundreds-of-thousands of new jobs. He generated $29 billion to finance new technologies and expansion in such firms as MCI, Time Warner, Twentieth Century Fox, Viacom and Turner Broadcasting.

HENRY MODELL (1892-1984) b. New York City
Merchant/Public Official Under his guidance, the company founded by his father grew into a major sporting goods and leisure wear chain with nineteen stores in the Metropolitan New York area. The late board chairman of Henry Modell & Company previously served our nation as a post-World War Two advisor to the U.S. Secretary of War on the disposal of surplus materials.

168

ARTHUR MURRAY (1895-1991) b. New York City
Dance Studio Entrepreneur The man who escorted millions of Americans onto dance floors devised simple step-by-step programs taught in coast-to-coast studios. His techniques were popularized by an eleven-year TV series and its theme song, "Arthur Murray Taught Me Dancing in a Hurry." His system graduated celebrities like Eleanor Roosevelt and John D. Rockefeller.

CHARLES REVSON (1906-75) b. Boston, MA
Beauty Products Corporate Leader A novel concept for its day, backed by persuasive advertising and promotion, energized the growth of Revlon Inc., one of America's leading cosmetic and fragrance firm. He introduced opaque nail enamels with matching lipsticks in 1939, and greatly diversified the company's beauty products during years of steady expansion around the globe.

JULIUS ROSENWALD (1862-1932) b. Springfield, IL
Merchant/Philanthropist He joined Chicago's Sears Roebuck & Company in 1895 and rose to its chairmanship which he held until his death. While at its helm, he piloted the mail order firm through years of dramatic countrywide growth. In the public interest, he financed YMCAs and schools for blacks, donating more than $30 million to such causes through the Julius Rosenwald Fund.

HELENA RUBINSTEIN (1871-1965) b. Cracow, Poland
Cosmetologist/Businesswoman The family formula for a modest facial cream – refined by the legendary patroness of beauty care – gave birth to a commercial empire. She constantly added items to her line during business expansions from Poland to Australia, London to Paris and then to New York in 1914. The hands-on entrepreneur personally created most of her 500 products.

169

MELVIN SIMON   (1928-) b. New York City
Business Leader In partnership with his brother, the son of a tailor is today the country's leading developer and manager of shopping malls. Melvin & Associates, founded in 1960, was worth more than $900 million at last report. He also produced several films in the 1970s, including *Love at First Bite*, and became co-owner of the Indiana Pacers basketball team in 1983.

NORTON SIMON   (1907-) b. Portland, OR
Industrialist/Philanthropist The food processing plant he acquired in 1932 was a springboard into other food-related businesses whose eventual net worth ranked among the nation's top one hundred corporations. He left in 1969 to dedicate full time to his several foundations which support culture and education. Los Angeles's Norton Simon art museum is among his gifts to America.

GERARD SWOPE   (1872-1957) b. St. Louis, MO
Industrialist The elder brother of journalist Herbert Bayard Swope achieved fame as chief executive of the General Electric Company (1922-39). In 1931 he issued the "Swope Plan" which invited industries to introduce practices that would reduce unemployment. He also served with distinction as an officer on the U.S. Army general staff during World War One.

LAURENCE TISCH   (1923-) b. New York City
Business Leader/Philanthropist His holding companies, Tisch Hotel chain and Loews Corporation, are parent organizations to a large network of companies in the insurance, shipping and entertainment industries. Considered an elder statesman in the business world, he has settled millions of charitable dollars on New York University and human welfare institutions.

LINDA WACHNER   (1946-)   b. New York City

Corporate Leader As president of Warnaco, Inc., a giant apparel conglomerate, she is counted among the nation's most successful businesswomen. A former department store salesperson, the self-made manager worked her way up through the industry and organized the buyout of her Fortune 500 company in 1986. She has since engineered its turnaround and return to profitability.

Other Noted Business Leaders

Louis Blaustein
– Founder of the American Oil Company and promotor of an early, advanced system of fuel distribution.

Harry and Richard Block
– Founders of H&R Block, the tax preparation service with street locations nationwide.

Edgar Bronfman
– American member of a distinguished family of Canadian industrialists and chief executive officer of Distillers Corporation, noted for his public service and philanthropic work.

Bennett Cohen and Jerry Greenfield
– Co-founders of the super-premium ice cream producer: Ben & Jerry's, a large corporate contributor to worthy causes.

Henry Dix
– Designer of the Red Cross uniform which became an international insignia, as well as U.S. Army and Navy nurse uniforms. At retirement he deeded his business to employees.

Maurice and Leon Falk
– Helped form the American Smelting and Refining Cor-

poration and founded a free University of Pittsburgh medical clinic for the poor.

Max Fisher
– Co-founder of the auto body production facility that tagged General Motors cars with its slogan "Body by Fisher," and former chairman of United Brands.

Arthur Frommer
– One of America's most popular travel guide writers, as well as a publisher and radio broadcaster.

Greenberg Brothers
– Founders of COLECO, an international toy company that created Cabbage Patch dolls and introduced the first mass-produced computer system for affordable, public use.

Gerald Greenwald
– Chairman of United Airlines, the country's largest employee-owned company. He was the industry's highest ranking Jewish executive when previously with Chrysler Motors.

Ruth and Elliot Handler
– Creators of the decade's most popular children's plaything: the internationally-distributed Barbie doll.

Leonard Jacoby and Stephen Meyers
– Partners in the noted legal firm, Jacoby & Meyers, which revolutionized legal practice through TV advertising and posted fees for services.

Joseph Kaplan
– Russian immigrant who inaugurated the age of brightly colored shower curtains.

Calvin Klein – Founder of a clothing and accessory fashion product house catering to a mass middle-class market.

Henry Kaufmann– Co-owner of Pittsburgh's foremost department store and donor of millions of philanthropic dollars.

J.K. Lasser
– Publisher over many years of America's most trusted and popular income tax preparation guides.

Samuel Leidesdorf
– Founder of one of the largest accounting firms in the nation, and a key figure in establishing the New York University Medical Center.

Gerald Levin
– Chairman of Time Warner, the world's largest media and entertainment conglomerate.

Alexander Levine
– President of a major development company owning shopping centers along the length of east coast, and a lavish donor to medical research, culture and education.

Stanley Marcus
– Founder and former chairman of Neiman-Marcus Company, the Dallas-based department story that set worldwide standards for elegance and exclusivity in quality merchandise.

Reuben Mattus
– The Polish immigrant and former candy store owner who introduced ice cream enthusiasts to Haagen-Dazs, the exotic original that spawned numerous imitations.

Jean Nidetch
– Founder of Weight Watcher's, the world's most popular weight loss system with a widely-sold line of dietetic foods.

Mo Ostin
– Former chief executive of Warner Brothers Records which became a multi-billion dollar sales leader in recorded music during his quarter-century rule.

Milton Petrie
– Late retail store chain owner and magnate, one of America's wealthiest men, who massively supported charitable causes.

Jay Pritzker
– A prominent member of the Chicago-based Pritzker business family, owners of Hyatt International Corporation and other industrial enterprises.

Vidal Sassoon
– Internationally-renowned hair stylist who became a leading business figure in the hair fashion and product industry.

Harry Scherman
– Joined Maxwell Sackheim and Robert Haas in forming the Book-of-the-Month Club in 1926.

Irving Shapiro
– Former chief executive of E.I. du Pont de Nemours & Co., the Delaware-based chemical giant.

James Shapiro
– Founder and president of the Simplicity Pattern Company, and mastermind of the home sewing industry.

Leonard Stern
– Chief executive officer of Hartz Mountain Industries.

Nathan Straus
– Co-owner of the Macy department store system, and noted philanthropist working on behalf of the nation's poor.

Roger Straus
– Founding co-partner and president of Farrar, Straus and Giroux Inc., a leading publishing firm.

Kurt Weishaupt
– President of a worldwide postage stamp wholesaling organization, named one of twelve most charitable U.S. citizens by America's Caring Institute in 1993.

Leslie Wexler
– Chief executive of the national chain of Limited Stores which pioneered the mass retail marketing of designer label fashions.

Elmer Winter
> – Co-founder of Manpower Inc., a leading national franchise for recruiting and placing temporary office and professional personnel.

Financial Industry Leaders

JULES BACHE (1862-1944) b. New York City
Financier/Philanthropist By age 30 he presided over a Wall Street bellwether, the banking firm of J.S. Bache & Company that led other financial interests into capitalizing America's future in transportation, manufacturing and insurance. Also a sophisticated art buyer, he deeded his valuable collection to New York City's Metropolitan Museum of Art.

OTTO KAHN (1867-1934) b. Mannheim, Germany
Financier/Philanthropist With his financial success as a partner in the banking firm of Kuhn, Loeb & Company, came generous support for music and the arts. He endowed museums, orchestras, art galleries and theaters. While chief executive officer and president of New York's Metropolitan opera (1903-31), he helped lift the institution to world-class status.

JAMES LOEB (1867-1933) b. New York City
Financier/Philanthropist He worked briefly in his father's financial firm, Kuhn, Loeb & Company before becoming an almost full-time benefactor to musical and educational programs. He founded music centers at Harvard and at New York City's Julliard Music Foundation. The Loeb Classical Library is also an institution of his making.

WALTER SACHS (1884-1980) b. New York City
Financier/Philanthropist The partner of Goldman, Sachs & Company, an international Wall Street banking firm, was the first Western banker of his stature to visit the Soviet Union to negotiate financial agreements (1925). He was deeply committed to civil rights programs, and joined in developing The National Association for the Advancement of Colored People (NAACP).

JACOB SCHIFF (1847-1920) b. Frankfort, Germany
Financier/Philanthropist Known for his financial wit and devotion to a booming America, the chief officer of Kuhn, Loeb and Company sought vast funding for many of the nation's newborn industries and railway systems. He was equally committed to worthy causes and was a major supporter of cultural, educational and human welfare organizations in the U.S. and abroad.

ERIC WARBURG (1900-90) b. Hamburg, Germany
Financier/Humanitarian The member of an illustrious international banking family fled his homeland in 1938 to assume the presidency of the New York banking organization bearing his name. During World War Two, he served as a much-decorated U.S. Army lieutenant colonel investigating Nazi war criminals. He helped relocate German scientists and their families in the West.

PAUL M. WARBURG (1868-1932) b. Hamburg, Germany
Financier/Public Official After joining his family's banking firm of M.M. Warburg and Company, he married the daughter of Solomon Loeb and settled in New York (1902). Subsequently, he and Senator Nelson Aldrich joined in reorganizing the U.S. banking system, resulting in the Glass-Owen Federal Reserve Board Act of 1913. He was appointed to the Fed's First board by President Woodrow Wilson.

Other Noted Financial Industry Leaders

Felix Warburg
– Member of the Warburg banking family who dedicated his life to supporting education, art and musical institutions.

James Wolfensohn
– Partner in the investment firm, Salomon Brothers, and a patron of the arts who helped raise the funds to refurbish Carnegie Hall on its centennial.

Advertising and Public Relations Executives

EDWARD L. BERNAYS (1891-) b. Vienna, Austria
Public Relations Pioneer The modernizer of his discipline was the first to use the phrase, "public relations counselors" to describe the role of P.R. professionals. The former journalist and publicist for entertainment celebrities was retained by blue chip corporations and major institutions. He set high standards for the field's ethical conduct and public responsibility.

WILLIAM BERNBACH (1911-82) b. New York City
Advertising Executive For more than twenty years he reigned as the owner and creative intelligence of one of the nation's top ten advertising agencies. Doyle Dane Bernbach helped transform the way products and services were promoted and marketed. Its outstanding campaigns billboarded such messages as "You don't have to be Jewish to Love Levy's (rye bread)."

ALBERT LASKER (1880-1952) b. Galveston, TX
Advertising Pioneer/Philanthropist His newspaper experience fed a passion for advertising which he brought to Lord & Thomas in 1898. Under his creative direction and eventual ownership, the Chicago agency ranked first in the world in stature and size. He also served America in a number of federal posts and formed the Lasker Foundation for medical research.

Other Noted Advertising and Public Relations Executives

Milton Biow
– Advertising agency owner and pioneer who, among other major concepts, created the "Call for Philip Morris" campaign.

Harold Burson
– Founder and chairman of Burson-Marsteller Inc., an international public relations agency.

Economists

KENNETH ARROW (1921-) b. New York City
Economist/Educator The Columbia University graduate was co-winner of a Nobel Prize for Economics in 1972. Earlier academic appointments included professorships in economics at Stanford University (1949-68) and at Harvard University (1968-79). His specialized field of study was the nature of collective choice when subjected to risk and uncertainty.

ARTHUR F. BURNS (1904-87) b. Stanislau, Austria
Economist/Government Official The key economic advisor to Presidents Dwight Eisenhower and Richard Nixon was appointed

to the Federal Reserve Board in 1970, and as U.S. ambassador to West Germany in 1981. His widely respected book *Measuring Business Cycles* (1946), written with W.C. Mitchell, is regarded to this day as a benchmark text for the world of business.

MILTON FRIEDMAN (1912-) b. New York City
Economist The outspoken and widely published member of the influential "Chicago School of Economics" is a leading advocate of monetary policy for a stable economy, opposing the Keynsian theory of government spending and stimulus. He proposes minimal interference by government in a free market system, and earned a 1976 Nobel Prize for Economics for evolving this theory.

ALAN GREENSPAN (1926-) b. New York City
Economist/Government Official He was appointed chairman of the Federal Reserve Board (1987) which has upheld his insistence on tightening the money supply to curb inflation. His counsel as economic advisor to the presidents strongly influenced the fiscal policies of the Richard Nixon, Gerald Ford, Ronald Reagan and George Bush administrations.

LAWRENCE KLEIN (1920-) b. Omaha, NE
Economist/Educator His analyses of the up-down patterns of business activity and the forces impinging on them won a Nobel Prize for Economics in 1980. His theories proposed reliable ways to predict shifts in the business climate. The college professor has written copiously on the subject and was President Carter's economic advisor from 1976 to 1981.

PAUL SAMUELSON (1915-) b. Gary, IN
Economist/Educator The Massachusetts Institute of Technology professor is recognized for his work in macro and mathematical

economics. A presentation of economic modeling appeared in his *Foundations of Economic Analysis* (1947), a study which in part earned a Nobel Prize for Economics in 1970. His other popular text is *Economics: An Introductory Analysis* (1947).

Among other leading Jewish-American economists of the century are:

Irving Fisher	**Benjamin Friedman**
Marshal Goldman	**Herbert Stein**
Murray Wiedenbaum.	

Labor Leaders

DAVID DUBINSKY (1892-1982) b. Brest-Litovsk, Byelorussia
Labor Union Leader The pioneering labor activist rose to the presidency of the International Ladies Garment Workers Union (ILGWU) in 1932. In a series of moves, he transferred the ILGWU from the American Federation of Labor (AFL) to the younger Congress of Industrial Organizations (CIO), and then returned it to the AFL in 1940. He was also a co-founder of New York's Liberal Party.

SAMUEL GOMPERS (1850-1924) b. London, England
Labor Union Leader Emigrating to the United States and settling in New York in 1863, the powerful union leader was central in energizing the labor movement by improving employer/employee relations and securing health and death benefits for workers. He helped organize the American Federation of Labor (AFL) in 1886, in which he was a key player until his death.

SIDNEY HILLMAN (1887-1946) b. Zagare, Lithuania
Labor Union Leader A former garment worker, he presided over the Amalgamated Clothing Workers of America from 1914 to 1946, and advocated an alliance between labor and management out of common interest. He was a catalyst for extensive reforms in union practices and industry relations, and was among the founders of the CIO which he served as vice president from 1935 to 1940.

JACKIE PRESSER (1926-88) b. Cleveland, OH
Labor Union Leader The gifted negotiator achieved a major coup in 1987 by merging the AFL, CIO and International Brotherhood of Teamsters into a single organization he headed since 1983. The consolidation closed a thirty-year union rift. He skillfully used the media to create a better understanding of the labor union's role in improving the lives of workers and their families.

Other Noted Labor Leaders

Sol Chaikin
– President of the International Ladies Garment Workers Union.

Murray Finley
– President of the Amalgamated Clothing and Textile Union of America.

Victor Gotbaum
– Former leader of New York City's largest public employee union: District Council 37.

Alex Rose
– Former president of the United Hat, Cap and Millinery Workers Union.

Albert Shanker
– President of the American Federation of Teachers and AFL-CIO vice president.

Ten
Sports

History recounts two Jewish sports heroes separated by 2,000 years: Ben Hur, the legendary athlete and charioteer of ancient Rome, and Daniel Mendoza, England's 1794 heavyweight champion who is hailed as the father of modern boxing. No Jewish sports figures of their stature emerged during the years between – although Hellenistic Jews participated and even prevailed in classic Greek events: discus throwing, marathon races and as gladiators.

Organized sports, as they are conducted today, were new to Western culture until the modern International Olympics were founded in 1896. But as competitive sports gained ground in American society, Jewish youth made its way into the arena and onto the field – despite a tradition which more greatly esteems careers in medicine, the law, education and science.

Young, athletically-inclined Jews seeking advancement were eager to escape the rough and tumble street life of New York and other large cities. Not only their natural abilities, but a fierce determination to excel, motivated the gifted athletes among them. From such origins came Jewish boxers who won championships in the 1920s and 1930s: Benny Leonard, Barney Ross and Ted Lewis dominated their field.

The 1920s also found growing numbers of Jewish students drawn to collegiate basketball; a few graduated to pro status. Of them, Nat Holman was a celebrated player and coach, and Red Auerbach was dubbed the crown prince of coaching.

New York's urban environment had also opened doors to casual sports for many Jewish youths – through pick-up games like handball, stickball and touch football which players outgrew.

But a handful did not outgrow them, and are today remembered as outstanding professionals of their games and times. Baseball's Hank Greenberg and Sandy Koufax. Football's Sid

Luckman, Marshall Goldberg and Sid Gilman. And swimming champion Mark Spitz whose seven gold medals set Olympic records.

If Jews were relatively scarce on the playing fields and courts, they continue to be prominent in management and coaching – and as founders of leagues, owners of teams, sports announcers and journalists. Above all as fans and spectators. Generations before, young Jews believed that sports appreciation was another certain way to Americanize. Their fascination with sports endures.

Sports Figures

MORRIS "MOE" BERG (1902-72) b. New York City
Baseball Player The accomplished athlete and scholar earned degrees from Princeton University and Columbia University's School of Law. After several years as a major league catcher, he was recruited by the U.S. government for espionage missions prior to World War Two. The charismatic adventurer who spoke twelve languages spied for the OSS, forerunner of the CIA.

BEN FRIEDMAN (1905-82) b. Cleveland, OH
Football Player "Friedman to Oosterban" was the catch phrase for football's first passing team powered by the arm of a great of his day. His fast release and pinpoint passing skewed football in the direction of more aerial play. The four-time All-Pro quarter-back spent seven years in the leagues, demonstrating that a combined passing-running game scores more points.

MARSHALL GOLDBERG (1917-) b. Elkins, WV
Football Player The steady hand in college and professional lineups was twice All-American with the University of Pittsburgh Panthers before joining the Chicago Cardinals in 1939. A strong runner and blocker during a solid eight-year pro career, the one-

time offensive fullback transferred his aggressive style to defensive play. He led the NFL in interceptions in 1941.

HENRY "HANK" GREENBERG (1911-86) b. New York City
Baseball Player Scoring 58 home runs during the 1938 season, the first Jewish Baseball Hall of Famer was only two long balls under Babe Ruth's world record. The Detroit Tigers' all-star outfielder (1933 to 1947) later played with the Pittsburgh Pirates and Cleveland Indians. He is ranked with the game's greatest right-hand hitters, with a lifetime .313 batting average.

SANDY KOUFAX (1935-) b. New York City
Baseball Pitcher At the peak of his game, the youngest player ever elected to the Baseball Hall of Fame enjoyed a brilliant five-year period that set major league records. He won an unprecedented three Cy Young Awards and pitched four no-hitters. The legendary manager, Casey Stengel, commented: "Forget Johnson, Waddele and Matthews, the Jewish kid was the best."

BENNY LEONARD (1896-1947) b. New York City
Boxer While ethnic gangs ranged the streets of lower Manhattan, the eleven-year old sidewalk brawler donned the gloves and won his first major bout in 1915. National fame followed his undisputed ownership of the world lightweight title from 1917 to 1924. The slugger with fast footwork scored 68 knockouts in 88 wins and is hailed as the all-time champion Jewish pugilist.

SID LUCKMAN (1916-) b. New York City
Football Player He was pivotal in replacing single wing field play with the modern T-formation. Signed on in 1939 by the Chicago Bears, he was the first quarterback to execute the dynamic "T" for a 73-0 upset of the Washington Redskins during the 1940 title

contest, transforming football forever. He also posted a record by tossing seven touchdown passes during a single game.

BARNEY ROSS (1909-67) b. New York City
Boxer The would-be Hebrew teacher altered plans and, by age eighteen, fought over 250 amateur bouts. Within six years he won the lightweight crown which he successfully defended five times. The canny body puncher also won a junior welterweight title, becoming the first to dominate both classes (1934-8). The film biography, *Monkey on my Back*, screened his victory over drug addiction.

MARK SPITZ (1950-) b. Modesto, CA
Olympic Swimmer During his competitive career (1965-72), the "World Swimmer of the Year" for 1967, 1971 and 1972 set 33 international records and brought home seven gold medals from the 1972 Munich Olympics. Each event was a record breaker by a superb athlete who, in the opinion of many aquatic sports experts, is the most outstanding swimmer the world has ever known.

Other Noted Sports Figures

Sidney Franklin
– The first professional Jewish bullfighter, born in Brooklyn, entered rings in Spain, Mexico, Portugal and South America.

Sid Gordon
– The dependable third baseman and solid hitter was a mainstay of the New York Giants.

Ernie Grunfeld
– A basketball player with a fierce competitive edge, he saw NBA action with the Milwaukee Bucks, Kansas City Kings and New York Knicks.

Johnny Kling

– The turn-of-the-century player was a ranking catcher of his day who helped spur the Chicago Cubs to its 1908 championship season.

Ronald Mix

– The hard-blocking San Diego Chargers offensive lineman played in seven all-star games during a stellar career that placed him in the Pro Football Hall of Fame.

Al Rosen

– The Cleveland Indians' third-baseman led the league in RBIs in 1952 and in 1953, the year he also slugged 43 home runs and won the MVP title by unanimous vote.

"Slapsie Maxie" Rosenbloom

– The colorful light heavyweight with a fleet-footed hit-and-run style held the class title from 1930 to 1934 before leaving for Hollywood and appearing in almost 100 films.

Richard Savitt

– Once said to be the game's finest backcourt tennis player, he was the first Jew to win at Wimbledon in singles competition.

Adolph Schayes

– Strong, quick and agile on the court, he set the pattern for basketball forwards, played for the Syracuse Nationals and retired to coach the Philadelphia 76ers.

Art Shamsky

– He spent eight years with the Cincinnati Reds and New York Mets as outfielder and first baseman, tying league records in 1966 with round-trippers at four consecutive times at bat.

Steve Stone

– A sharp breaking curve was the money pitch of the 1980 Cy Young award winner on the mound for the Baltimore Orioles. After retirement, he went on to become a sports broadcaster.

Owners, Managers Coaches and Executives

ARNOLD "RED" AUERBACH (1917-) b. New York City
Basketball Coach The most successful basketball coach in history began his career in 1946 with the Washington franchise of the original Basketball Association of America. He since led the Boston Celtics to nine NBA titles and was instrumental in bringing black Americans into the game: Chuck Cooper, the first to play in the NBA, and Bill Russell, the first to coach a pro league team.

AL DAVIS (1929-) b. Brockton, MA
Football Commissioner During the past thirty years he served as a player, coach and owner, and was appointed commissioner of the American Football League in 1966. As head coach and general manager of the Oakland Raiders, which later moved to Los Angeles, he led his team to its most consistently successful franchise, goaded on by his memorable words: "Just win, baby!"

BARNEY DREYFUSS (1865-1932) b. Freiberg, Germany
Baseball Owner The general manager and owner of the Pittsburgh Pirates inaugurated the first World Series in 1903 when his team played the Boston Pilgrims of the American League. With the exception of 1904 and 1994, baseball never missed an annual series. The astute and hard-driving sports executive also contributed to the inception of pro football.

SIDNEY GILLMAN (1911-) b. Minneapolis, MN
Football Coach Entering pro football as head coach of the Los Angeles Rams (1955), he was reputed for innovations on the gridiron. He championed the forward pass and worked it into play strategy, which added more offensive punch to college and pro football. He also helped develop the two platoon system and was elected to the Professional Football Hall of Fame.

187

EDDIE GOTTLIEB (1898-1979) b. Kiev, Russia
Basketball Coach/Executive Professional basketball credits the Philadelphia Warriors' owner and coach (1956-62) with helping wean the game from its infancy. The manager joined in forming the Basketball Association of America (1946) which evolved into the National Basketball Association. He entered the Basketball Hall of Fame for outstanding contributions to the sport.

NAT HOLMAN (1896-1994) b. New York City
Basketball Coach The versatile player during his collegiate years advanced to coach formidable teams at the City College of New York (1920-53) and sporadically after. During the Twenties, he doubled as a player with the original Celtics, boosting their victorious seasons. The game tactician also devised the pivot play and crowned his coaching career with a 422/188 win/loss tally.

WILLIAM "RED" HOLZMAN (1920-) b. New York City
Basketball Coach The court savvy of the former college All-American guided the New York Knicks to its finest years – NBA championships in 1970 and 1973. During the decade he handled the Knicks (1967-77), the team broke league records with a lifetime total of 696 victories – second only to "Red" Auerbach's Boston Celtics. He was elected to the Basketball Hall of Fame in 1985.

HIRSCH JACOBS (1904-70) b. New York City
Horse Trainer A field of sports seldom associated with Jewish participants had its past master in a horse breeder and trainer whose thoroughbreds hit the wire on the money 3,569 times – a record that still stands. His savvy and patience in nurturing prospects to track readiness, netted over $12 million for stables which bet on his horse sense.

MIKE JACOBS (1880-1953) b. New York City

Boxing Promoter The foremost boxing promotor of his day was outstanding at drawing crowds and prime news coverage to his events. He typically staged contests for heavyweight champion Joe Lewis which at one time drew a million-dollar gate, a record-breaker of its day. He also founded the 20th Century Sporting Club in the 1930s.

MARV LEVY (1928-) b. Chicago, IL

Football Coach Recognized as one of the most capable and committed coaches in the game, he led the NFL Buffalo Bills to four straight Super Bowls (1992-95). He previously skippered the Kansas City Chiefs, turning the squad around for a divisional third-place finish in 1981. The Phi Betta Kappa history major helped make team history as a solid game planner favoring defense and kicking.

MAURICE PODOLOFF (1890-1985) b. Elizabethgrad, Russia

Football Executive During the year he retired as president of the American Hockey League (1946), the attorney helped organize the basketball league later named the NBA. Accepting its presidency, he was instrumental in introducing the 24-second clock and airing games on TV since 1954. These moves galvanized play and helped lift the sport to its present day stature.

ABE SAPERSTEIN (1903-66) b. London, England

Basketball Owner His skills as a sports entrepreneur and show-man helped win countless fans around the world for American basketball. He formed an all-black team in 1927 – the now legen-dary Harlem Globetrotters – and coached it into hilarious play. Every game was a carnival on the court. Nevertheless, the team was a serious contender which won the 1940 world championship.

AL SCHACHT (1892-1984) b. New York City

Baseball's Prankster "The Clown Prince of Baseball" amused millions attending games in the major and minor leagues, and entertained U.S. troops during World War Two. A pantomimist and jester, he had pitched during his early career for the Washington Senators (1919-21) before a sore arm forced his retirement. He eventually opened a popular New York City restaurant bearing his name.

DAVID STERN (1942-) b. New York City

Basketball Executive The commissioner of the National Basketball Association since 1984 devised marketing techniques that transformed the league from an "also ran" into a successful venture with worldwide reputation. A $10 million bonus from grateful team owners coincided with his being named the Executive of the Decade by the Associated Press (1989).

Other Contributors to the American Way of Sports

Larry Brown
– The former player specialized in turning around losing basketball teams while varsity coach at UCLA, and while coaching the Denver Nuggets and Indiana Pacers.

Irving Felt
– The businessman and sports impresario led a 1960's drive to build a new Madison Square Garden. The complex's Felt Forum was named in his honor.

Marvin Miller
– A major figure in the game's recent history, he organized the baseball Players Association and brought free agency to the sport.

190

Max Novich
 – Regarded as the dean of sports medicine, the decorated World War Two surgeon is a crusader for contact sport safety and founder of New Jersey's famed Sports Injury Center.

Max Patkin
 – The hilarious basketball court clown performs during period breaks somewhat in the style of Al Schacht.

David "Sonny" Werblin
 – In addition to acquiring Joe Namath who quarterbacked the New York Jets to a championship, the team's ex-owner was an architect of the merger that formed the NFL.

Among other prominent Jewish-American executives in pro football are:

Leon Hess
 – owner of the New York Jets

Carroll Rosenbloom
 – owner of the Los Angeles Rams

Robert Preston Tisch
 – co-owner of the New York Giants

Sportswriters and Sportscasters

MARV ALBERT (1943-) b. New York City
Sportscaster During the past two decades, he has established himself as one of television's premier play-by-play game announcers in basketball, hockey and football. He was the original play caller on radio and TV for the New York Knicks and the New York Rangers. In addition, he provided his brand of lively and sharp coverage for the New York Giants.

MEL ALLEN (1913-) b. Birmingham, AL
Sportscaster "Going, going, gone," was a gift to the vocabulary of reportage by a radio personality whose eloquence, wit and talent set lively standards for sports broadcasting since his 1936 debut on CBS. The genial Voice of the New York Yankees also manned the microphones at more than sixty World Series, Baseball All Star and championship bowl games.

HOWARD COSELL (1920-95) b. Winston-Salem, NC
Sportscaster He became the best known and most visible personality on mike during the growth of organized sports from the 1950s through the Eighties. The popularizer of Monday night football was a leading figure in establishing professional football as America's emerging number-one game. He was also credited with burnishing the image of boxing champion Mohammed Ali.

NAT FLEISCHER (1887-1972) b. New York City
Editor/Boxing Promoter The founder of *Ring* magazine and author of more than sixty books was often cited as the century's most influential figure in boxing. His publication provided universal boxing coverage, official ratings, as well as the concept of championship belts. "Mr. Boxing," as he was called, also helped organize boxing commissions around the world.

MARTY GLICKMAN (1917-) b. New York City
Sportscaster A talented athlete in his youth, he was forced off the U.S. track team at the 1936 Berlin Olympics by Nazi authorities, and was replaced by Jesse Owens. For the past fifty years, he broadcast New York football and basketball games, and became an esteemed mentor to his colleagues in the news booths. Many fondly regard him as the dean of local play-by-play.

192

Other Noted Sportswriters and Sportscasters

Roger Kahn
– author of the baseball classic, *The Boys of Summer*

Leonard Koppett
– sports columnist for *The New York Times*

Bill Mazer
– former TV sportscaster with encyclopedic memory

Shirley Povich
– sports columnist for *The Washington Post.*

Dick Young
– late sports columnist for *The New York Daily News*

Recreational

BOBBY FISCHER (1943-) b. Chicago, IL
Chess Player An enigmatic figure surrounded by controversy, he parleyed his strategic genius at the chessboard into a U.S. championship at age fifteen. By 1958 he was promoted to the rank of international grandmaster and brought home the 1972 world chess championship. His refusal to compete against Russian Jew Anatoly Karpov in 1975 returned the award to the USSR.

Among other Jewish-American world-class chessmasters are:

Reuben Fine   **Emanuel Lasker**
Samuel Resevsky   **William Steinitz**

CHARLES GOREN (1901-91) b. Philadelphia, PA
Bridge Master He abandoned the law for his first love, contract bridge, and did more than any writer, columnist or lecturer in his field to propagate the game in America. His system of allocating

points for honor cards and suit distribution is nearly universal. He wrote more than fifty books, including the bestseller *Contract Bridge Complete* (1951).

FRED LEBOW (1932-94) b. Arad, Romania
Runner The founder and guiding spirit of the New York City Marathon was credited with popularizing long distance running in the U. S. He ran in the city's first marathon in 1970, competing with only 55 runners. By 1993, the New York event he inspired attracted more than 26,000 contestants. He was inducted into the National Track and Field Hall of Fame in 1994.

Eleven
Jewish Institutions, Philanthropies and Organizations

Jewish contributions to the well-being of our nation's way of life is visible from coast to coast. It is seen in hospitals, medical research centers, libraries, museums and YMHAs. The Jewish founders, operators and supporters of these institutions which serve all Americans, join hands with their neighbors in the spirit of brotherhood and good citizenship.

Today we find more than fifty U.S. hospitals and medical centers built and chiefly supported by Jewish philanthropies and organizations. Among the facilities are:

Leo N. Levi National Arthritis Hospital	Hot Springs Park, AR
Sun Air Federation and Home for Asthmatic Children	Beverly Hills, CA
Cedars-Sinai Medical Center	Los Angeles, CA
Jewish National Hospital at Denver	Los Angeles, CA
Sinai Medical Center	Los Angeles, CA
Mount Zion Hospital & Medical Center	San Francisco, CA
Hope Center for the Retarded	Denver, CO
Jewish National Home-Home for Asthmatic Children	Denver, CO
National Jewish Center for Immunology and Respiratory Medicine	Denver, CO

National Jewish Hospital & Research Center-National Asthma Center	Denver, CO
National Jewish Hospital/National Asthma Center	Denver, CO
Cancer Research Center & Hospital	Lakewood, CO
Mount Sinai Hospital	Hartford, CT
Michael Reese Hospital & Medical Center	Chicago, IL
Schwab Rehabilitation Center	Chicago, IL
The Ark	Chicago, IL
Jewish Hospital	Louisville, KY
Touro Infirmary	New Orleans, LA
Beth Israel	Boston, MA
Levindale Hebrew Geriatric Center & Hospital	Baltimore, MD
Sinai Hospital of Detroit	Detroit, MI
Mount Sinai Hospital of Minneapolis	Minneapolis, MN
Menorah Medical Center	Kansas City, MO
Jewish Hospital	St. Louis, MO
Jewish Hospital & Rehabilitation Center of New Jersey	Jersey City, NJ
Newark Beth Israel Medical Center	Newark, NJ
Albert Einstein College Hospital	Bronx, NY

Albert Einstein College of Medicine of Yeshiva University	Bronx, NY
Beth Abraham Hospital	Bronx, NY
Hebrew Hospital for Chronic Sick	Bronx, NY
Brookdale Hospital Medical Center	Brooklyn, NY
Kingsbrook Jewish Medical Center	Brooklyn, NY
Maimonides Medical Center	Brooklyn, NY
Mount Sinai Hospital-City Hospital at Elmhurst Affiliate	Elmhurst, NY
Long Island Jewish-Hillside Medical Center	New Hyde Park, NY
Albert Einstein College of Medicine of Yeshiva University	New York, NY
Beth Israel Medical Center	New York, NY
Beth Israel Medical Center-Alcoholism Treatment Program	New York, NY
Jewish Memorial Hospital	New York, NY
The Mount Sinai Medical Center	New York, NY
The Jewish Hospital of Cincinnati	Cincinnati, OH
The Mount Sinai Medical Center	Cleveland, OH
Eagleville Hospital & Rehabilitation Center	Eagleville, PA
Montefiore Hospital	Pittsburgh, PA
The Miriam Hospital	Providence, RI

Mount Sinai Medical Center   Milwaukee, WI

More than 900 community-based YMHAs from coast-to-coast are cultural centers with myriad programs in adult education, the graphic and performing arts, and recreation and fitness. In a typical example, the prominent 92nd Street YMHA in Manhattan has become a choice center for New York City's intellectual and cultural life.

We also find an age-old tradition of philanthropy governing thousands of Jewish foundations and groups which in 1993 gave approximately 10% of the over $12 billion total donated by all U.S. charitable organizations – a disproportionately high rate compared with that of other sources of giving. Among the recipients of Jewish organization grants, regardless of religious, racial or ethnic affiliations are:

> Animal-specific agencies
> Arts and humanities organizations
> Churches and temples
> Civil rights groups
> Colleges and Universities
> Community improvement groups
> Disease-specific health associations
> Educational support agencies
> Environmental agencies
> Federated funds
> Government agencies
> Graduate schools
> Hospitals and medical care facilities
> Human service agencies
> Information and public education centers
> International organizations
> Junior and community colleges
> Libraries
> Media organizations

Medical research institutes
Mental health agencies
Museums and historical societies
Performing arts groups
Philanthropic organizations
Professional societies and associations
Public administration agencies
Public and general health organizations
Recreation organizations
Research institutes
Schools
Social science organizations
Technical assistance centers
Youth development organizations

Tolerance and a respect for civil liberties are deeply rooted in Jewish consciousness and activism. Since 1906, the American Jewish Committee (AJC) has worked to realize the freedoms and human rights granted by our Constitution and laws. Recognizing the threat to our principles and traditions by anti-semitism, racism and bigotry, the AJC promotes harmony and understanding in alliance with other religions and ethnic groups. *The New York Times* affirms the AJC is "the dean of Jewish civil and human rights organizations."

The B'nai B'rith is another leading public service organization which stated its purpose in words that apply to others like it. Its objectives are to join in " . . . inculcating the purist principles of philanthropy, honor and patriotism, of supporting science and art, of alleviating the wants of the poor and needy, of visiting and caring for the sick, of coming to the rescue of victims of persecution, and of providing for, protecting and assisting the aged, the widow and the orphan on the broadest principles of humanity."

The UJA-Federation, an equally important organization, funds 130 human and social service programs in more than fifty countries worldwide. It provides help as needed, "making a real difference in the lives of 4.5 million people, one at a time." Hundreds of other national Jewish organizations like them provide community services with wide outreach. Among the better known are:

American Jewish Committee Institute of Human Relations	New York, NY
American Jewish Congress	New York, NY
Anti-defamation League of B'nai B'rith	New York, NY
Conference of Presidents of Major American Jewish Organizations	New York, NY
Consultative Council of Jewish Organizations	New York, NY
Coordinating Board of Jewish Organizations	Washington, DC
Council of Jewish Organizations in Civil Service	New York, NY
Jewish Labor Committee Atran Center for Jewish Culture	New York, NY
Jewish Peace Fellowship	Nyack, NY
Jewish War Veterans of the United States of America	Washington, DC
National Association of Jewish Legislators	Slingerlands, NY
National Jewish Coalition	Washington, DC
National Jewish Commission on Law and Public Affairs	New York, NY
National Jewish Democratic Council	Washington, DC

World Conference of Jewish Communal Services	Kendall Park, NJ
World Jewish Congress	New York, NY
American Biblical Encyclopedia Society	Monsey, NY
Congress for Jewish Culture	New York, NY
Jewish Academy of Arts and Sciences	New York, NY
Jewish Book Council	New York, NY
National Foundation for Jewish Culture	New York, NY
Hadassah the Women's Zionist Organization of America	New York, NY
American Jewish Joint Distribution Committee	New York, NY
United Jewish Appeal	New York, NY
B'nai B'rith Hillel Foundations	Washington, DC
Congress of Secular Jewish Organizations	Chicago, IL
Council of Jewish Federations	New York, NY

Judaism holds that giving is twice rewarded: as a gift to the recipient and as a satisfaction to oneself. By reaching out in decency and friendship to fellow citizens, the nation's Jews celebrate their role in the building of America.

201

Twelve
The Yiddish-English Connection

The estimated 615,000 words in its vocabulary make English the most nimble of history's 3,000 or more languages. Yet English continues to adopt foreign words and expressions for which it has no counterparts. And it has a special affinity for Yiddish, a 1,000 year-old tongue concocted mostly from German with a smattering of Hebrew, Slavic and Romance languages.

Nowhere but in Yiddish would you find a more colorful or pungent collection of words with the sense of *chutzpa, kosher, plotz* and *klutz*. The invasion of idiomatic Yiddish into everyday speech largely traces to America's exposure to popular Jewish authors and comedians. And if you are a *mavin*, not a *kibitzer*, you should easily translate many of these without a *glitch*.

Where underlined, the ch *is sounded gutturally by closing the back of the throat.*

Bagel - hard, glazed roll resembling a doughnut

Baleboste - expert and dominant head of a household

Bar Mitzvah - ceremony at age 13 conferring duties of manhood

Bialy - soft onion roll depressed in its center

Bissel - little bit or small amount

Blintz - rolled-up pancake enclosing cottage cheese or fruit

Borsht - beet soup

Boychik - fond expression for a boy or a man

Bubbe-Mayse - ludicrous story or old wive's tale

Bubeleh - affectionate term shared by couples, family and friends

Challa - braided loaf of glazed white bread

Chalootz - pioneer (early settler in Palestine)

Chasid - member of an orthodox Jewish sect

Chozzer - hoggish, greedy or mean-spirited person

Chutzpa - audacity, impudence or cheekiness

Daven - to pray
Dreck - rubbish, shoddy or useless
Fablunget - befuddled or bewildered
Famisht - muddled or mixed up
Fatumelt - rattled or confused
Feh - exclamation of disgust or rejection
Gelt - money, assets
Gevalt - exclamation of shock, disbelief or horror
Gezunt-heit - response to a sneeze ("Be healthy")
Ghetto - Jewish quarter within a city
Glitch - slip or mistake
Goniff - thief, unscrupulous or devious person
Haymish - homelike, comfortable, friendly
Halleluyah - "Praise be to the Lord"
Ipsy-pipsy - "All is well"
Ish Kabibble - "Who cares?" or "No matter"
K'nocker - notable or accomplished person
Kibbutznick - member of an Israeli *kibbutz* (settlement)
Kibitzer - wisecracker, prankster or teaser
Kishkeh - guts, intestines
Klutz - bumbling, awkward or insensitive person
Kosher - in accord with dietary laws, or genuine, sincere
Kreplach - small dumplings filled with cheese or meat
Kvell - glow with joy, pride or self-satisfaction
Kvetch - a complainer or to complain, to squeeze
L'chayim - toast before taking a drink ("To life")
Lox - Smoked salmon, saltier than "Novie"
    (Nova Scotia salmon)
Luft-mench - impractical visionary, starry-eyed or
    naive person
Matzoh - unleavened bread of the Hebrews escaping Egypt
Mavin - proficient, authoritative or knowledgeable person
Mazel - luck, good fortune

Mazel Tov - "Good luck," "It's about time" or "Congratulations"

Megilla - routine, dull or drawn-out business

Menorah - nine-branch candelabra

Mentsh - exemplary, splendid or significant person

Meshugge - crazy, tormented or eccentric

Mishmosh - mess, foul-up or chaos

Mitzvah - sacred duty or thoughtful act

Nebish - impotent, hapless or feeble nobody

No-goodnyick - worthless, untrustworthy or dishonest rascal

Nosh - quick snack or light meal

Omeyn - Jewish form of Amen recited after prayer ("So be it")

Oy - all-purpose utterance like "Oh", "Wow" or "Woe is me"

Paskudnyack - repulsive, nasty, grasping or sly person

Passover - eight days celebrating Hebrew's release from slavery

Plotz- blow up, erupt or collapse in a seat

Pogrom - organized, violent attack against Jewish communities

Pushke - container for charitable contributions

Putz - obscene sexual innuendo aimed at a dunce or blockhead

Rabbi - Jewish clergyman and teacher

Saychel- intelligence, smarts

Schmaltz - sentimentality, gushiness or fat used in cooking

Shabbes - Sabbath

Shalom - "Hello," "Good-by" or "Peace"

Shikker - intoxicated

Shiksa - non-Jewish female

Shlemazel - luckless person for whom everything fails

Shlemeel - fool whose constant failures are self-inflicted

Shlep - drag along, carry, a lazy person or slob

Shlock - inferior, phony, tacky or cheap looking

Shlub - clumsy, uncouth or crude person

Shmatte - rag, trash or cheap quality

Shmeer - spread or ladle on, or to bribe

Shmendrick - similar to *nebish* or *shlemeel*

Shmo - similar to *shmendrick*

Shmootz - dirt, filth

Shmooz - amiable or idle talk, or personal chat

Shmuck - similar to *putz*

Shnaps - hard liquor or other spirits

Shnook - similar to *nebish* or *shlemeel*

Shnorer - moocher or swindler, or insolent beggar

Shnoz - oversized or disfiguring nose

Shofer - ram's horn sounded in synagogues during high holy days

Shool - synagogue

Shpritz - sprinkle, spray or drizzle

Shtup - shove, push or vulgar form for having sexual intercourse

Shvartz - dark, foreboding

Tchatchke - toy or cheap knickknack, or a loose woman

Toches - backside, buttocks

Torah - first five books of the bible (Pentateuch)

Treyf - non-Kosher or "unclean" food

Tsadik - virtuous, devout or saintly man

Tsidaka - charitable giving

Tsores - miseries, predicaments, problems or hardships

Tumler - noisy, boisterous or disruptive person

Tush - posterior

Vuden - "What then?" or "What else do you expect?

Yarmulke - skullcap

Yeshiva - Hebrew school from primary to collegiate level

Yontif - religious holiday, special observance or festivity

Zaftik - juicy, plump, chesty or sexually desirable woman

JEWISH-AMERICAN NOBEL PRIZE
WINNERS (1907-90)

Nobel Prize for Physics

Albert Michelson (1907)
Otto Stern (1943)
Isidor Rabi (1944)
Felix Bloch (1952)
Donald Glaser (1960)
Richard Hofstadter (1961)
Richard Feynman (1965)
Julian Schwinger (1965)
Hans Bethe (1967)
Murray Gell-Mann (1969)
Burton Richter (1976)
Arno Penzias (1978)
Sheldon Glashow (1979)
Steven Weinberg (1979)
Leon Lederman (1988)
Melvin Schwartz (1988)
Jack Steinberger (1988)
Jerome Friedman (1990)

Nobel Prize for Physiology or Medicine

Karl Landsteiner (1930)
Joseph Erlanger (1944)
Hermann Muller (1946)
Gerty Cory (1947)
Selman Waksman (1952)
Fritz Lipmann (1953)
Joshua Lederberg (1958)

206

Arthur Kornberg (1959)
Konrad Bloch (1964)
George Wald (1967)
Marshall Nirenberg (1968)
Salvador Luria (1969)
Julius Axelrod (1970)
Gerald Edelman (1972)
David Baltimore (1975)
Howard Temin (1975)
Baruch Blumberg (1976)
Rosalyn Yalow (1977)
Daniel Nathans (1978)
Baruj Benacceraf (1980)
Michael Brown (1985)
Joseph Goldstein (1985)
Stanley Cohen (1986)
Rita Levi-Montalcini (1986)
Gertrude Elion (1988)
Harold Varmus (1989)

Nobel Prize for Chemistry

Melvin Calvin (1961)
William Stein (1972)
Herbert Brown (1979)
Paul Berg (1980)
Walter Gilbert (1980)
Roald Hoffmann (1981)
Sidney Altman (1989)

Nobel Prize for Peace

Henry Kissinger (1973)
Elie Wiesel (1986)

Nobel Prize for Literature

Saul Bellow (1976)
Isaac Bashevis Singer (1978)
Joseph Brodsky (1987)

Nobel Prize for Economics

Paul Samuelson (1970)
Simon Kuznets (1971)
Kenneth Arrow (1972)
Milton Friedman (1976)
Herbert Simon (1978)
Lawrence Klein (1980)
Robert Solow (1987)
Harry Markowitz (1990)

ABOUT THE AUTHORS

Asher B. Etkes has pioneered various firsts during a lifetime career in business and industry. An architect by training, he formed the first public relations firm specializing in counseling professionals, and co-founded the nation's first company offering color negatives for newspaper printing. He also created special playgrounds for able and disabled children who learn through successful movement and games, and organized the first manufacturer of unique modular containment systems for environmental protection. Mr. Etkes has written and lectured on early years' educational development through physical play and on public relations and marketing issues.

Saul Stadtmauer is a published author with a background in journalism and public relations. Among his titles are works on human development, personal finance, military history and in the children's book field. He has also written feature articles, speeches, video scripts and newsletters for Fortune 500 companies, educational and health institutions, philanthropic groups, communications services and diverse professional, business and industrial organizations.

REQUEST TO READERS

We invite you to help make *Jewish Contributions to the American Way of Life* an ever-growing testimony to notable achievements of men and women of Jewish origin who have lived or live now in 20th Century America.

Your suggestions of people to add to our second edition are welcome. Please send copies of *reliable and complete* background information from which we might draft brief biographies.

If our editors select one or more of your submissions for publication, your name will appear on the acknowledgement page of the forthcoming edition. Please mail your nominations to:

The Editors, Jewish Contributions/Northside Publishing, Inc.
41-04 35th Avenue, Long Island City, NY 11101

INDEX